T0339973

The Impostor Leaders

Taking a novel approach to the subject of leadership, this book uses its dark side as a vehicle to highlight some important leadership lessons, helping all managers to reflect on their own performance.

The Impostor Leaders clarifies what is meant by genuine leadership, focusing on the fact that leading and managing go hand in hand. Based on this ability to consistently combine the leadership and management roles, this book describes in detail and practical terms, using real-world examples, the range of good and bad leader-types seen in organizations today. The Leadership Wheel is also introduced as a conceptual framework to isolate eight types of leaders across four categories.

Appealing to leaders and managers across industry sectors, this book's substantial analysis of bad leadership gives readers a tangible framework against which to consider their own capabilities.

Enda M. Larkin is an entrepreneur, manager, and consultant with over 30 years' international experience across multiple business sectors. He is author of five management books and his first novel, *Into the Fire*, was published in 2020. Follow him at www.endalarkin.net.

The Impostor Leaders

Lessons on How Not to Lead

Enda M. Larkin

Routledge
Taylor & Francis Group

NEW YORK AND LONDON

First published 2021
by Routledge
52 Vanderbilt Avenue, New York, NY 10017

and by Routledge
2 Park Square, Milton Park, Abingdon, Oxon OX14 4RN

Routledge is an imprint of the Taylor & Francis Group, an informa business

Library of Congress Cataloging-in-Publication Data
Names: Larkin, Enda M., author.
Title: The impostor leaders : lessons on how not to lead / Enda M. Larkin.
Description: New York, NY : Routledge, 2021. | Includes bibliographical references and index.
Identifiers: LCCN 2020044072 (print) | LCCN 2020044073 (ebook) |
Subjects: LCSH: Leadership. | Management.
Classification: LCC HD57.7 L3688 2021 (print) | LCC HD57.7 (ebook) |
DDC 658.4/092--dc23
LC record available at https://lccn.loc.gov/2020044072
LC ebook record available at https://lccn.loc.gov/2020044073

ISBN: 978-0-367-64976-0 (hbk)
ISBN: 978-0-367-64973-9 (pbk)
ISBN: 978-1-003-12724-6 (ebk)

Typeset in Sabon
by Taylor & Francis Books

For Keeva and Emily Larkin
My inspiration. My joy. My life.

Contents

Illustrations

Figures

Tables

Preface

"My boss really hates me." Those were his opening words. Then, clearly unhappy, this likeable and competent (if somewhat timid) young manager proceeded to catalogue the daily abuse he suffered from his boss. It was not just the constant sarcasm and snide remarks. Nor was it the frequent personal attacks on him in front of others. It was not even the unnecessary denigration of his work just to show him who was in charge that got to him. No, he could struggle through all of that and the rest. It was, he said, the sense of helplessness that was hardest to take. That and the loss of self-esteem he was feeling because of his inability to stand up to his boss.

Maybe your first reaction is that this young man should have been a bit more assertive and stood up for himself. And, yes, he probably should have done. You might also be thinking that he could have just jumped ship but with small kids and a big mortgage his mobility was restricted. He might even have reported his boss, although ambition and the fear of being labelled a troublemaker meant that doing so would only ever be a last resort. In fact, it would be easy to blame him for his own circumstances.

And that is often what happens because there is still a tendency to fault the victim, not the aggressor. Frequently, the undertone of the message to people like him is, "Have you no backbone?" This completely misses the point, and that sort of attitude only shifts the blame away from where it belongs. It is the failings of the leader that should warrant the attention, not the other way around. Working for a boss from hell can be soul-destroying. They wreak havoc as they demoralize and dishearten, intimidate and insult, or criticize and coerce. Left unchecked they stifle rather than stimulate employee engagement causing untold if at times hidden damage to organizational and individual performance. Nobody deserves to suffer under a lousy leader, yet for many people it remains an everyday reality.

I want to be very clear about something from the start. I am not, repeat *not*, talking here about managers who get it wrong occasionally, lose their cool every now and again, or lack some of the required qualities and skills to lead effectively. That is natural and indeed only human; nobody is perfect after all and everyone gets it wrong from time to time. What I am referring to are those individuals who fail the leadership challenge, not just occasionally but continuously. I am talking about the Impostor Leaders.

Calling them Impostors might seem a bit dramatic. But if you really think about it that is precisely what they are. They are fakes, pure and simple; wolves in sheep's clothing, you might even say, so the label is well suited. Sure, they may pose as authentic leaders, holding the right titles and saying all the right things yet they are far from the real deal. In truth, they are living a lie, often without even realizing it, because the way they think and act much of the time is the antithesis of genuine leadership. Not all Impostors harm to the same degree, of course. Some merely frustrate by their incompetence or negativity, whereas others inflict real and prolonged pain on those who report to them. Regardless of their severity, what distinguishes Impostor Leaders is that their poor performance is unremitting, not intermittent. For them, getting it wrong is the rule, not the exception.

During my 30-year career as an entrepreneur, manager, and consultant I have encountered more than my fair share of these Impostors. They completely wind me up, I must admit, and my blood pressure goes through the roof every time I am exposed to their ineptitude, or when I see the harsh treatment that some of them dish out to their employees. What I find most astounding, though, is how many of these Impostor Leaders not only survive their poor performance but can even prosper in certain organizations. It is beyond belief in the modern world, yet it still happens all the time. That said, I never intended to write a book about them. In fact, nothing was further from my mind. To me, they were simply one of the downsides to working life and people either had to learn to deal with them or move on. Until recently, I had no real interest in the Impostors other than they provided great source material on how not to lead.

That has now changed. I have increasingly come to realize that the Impostor Leaders do not only damage those who work under them. That is bad enough for starters, and worthy of scrutiny. But they can also have a negative impact on their peers as well. Increasingly, I have noticed how they poison the atmosphere at work or how some of them, directly and indirectly, influence the behavior of other managers around them. If allowed, and often they are, the worst of the Impostors can create a working environment where seeking to apply positive leadership approaches is viewed as a weakness rather than a strength. Like some organizational virus, the shortcomings seen in these anti-leaders tend to spread, if left unchecked. That was not something to be ignored indefinitely.

The final straw about the Impostors came for me when I heard that young manager say the words "My boss really hates me" as he looked for advice one evening on a residential training program. There was not really anything particularly unique about his story, I had seen and heard similar cases many times before, but there was a real sense of despair in the way he told it; must have been something in his tone of voice that did it. Whatever it was, I decided enough was enough. That night, the Impostor Leaders was born.

The Impostor Leaders is most definitely not a book about 'boss bashing.' Being a leader is never easy, nor is it possible to get it right every time. This I know from first-hand experience and like every other manager I made plenty of mistakes along the way. It is, however, about recognizing that while there are many great leaders around – celebrated and unheralded – who make a positive difference to their employees' daily experience, there are plenty of the Impostors too; far too many of them if you ask me. The majority of leadership books focus on the positive, uplifting potential of leaders and I am all for that but the alter-ego of leadership – the Mr Hyde to Dr Jekyll's pleasant façade – does not get nearly enough attention given its prevalence.

This book focuses on that shadow side of authority and power practiced by the Impostor Leaders. It does so not as a tirade against them for although therapeutic and, dare I say it enjoyable, that would not be very constructive. Nor is the content here a detailed examination of the growing body of research that is highlighting the extent and consequences of the problem. Neither does it provide coping strategies. Rather, the primary intention of this book is to explore the world of Impostors as a means of helping all managers to reflect on their own leadership performance. The late Jack Welch once said, "I've learned that mistakes can often be as good a teacher as success,"[1] and there is certainly plenty to be learned from the short-comings seen in the Impostor Leaders. Rarely, if ever, are their failings used as the main vehicle for learning, so this book is unique in that respect. It focuses on what not to do as a means of helping you to identify your own areas for improvement.

Whatever your existing title or level on the management ladder, whether you are just starting out or sitting at the top of the tree, whether you work in a start-up or a state body, the Impostor Leaders will help you to consider your own talents in light of the failings of others. The intention here is not to teach, or indeed to preach; rather this book offers you a chance, in a non-judgemental way, to reflect on your current capabilities. It provides valuable food for thought as to why striving to be the best leader you can is always the better option over the long term.

Note

1 Jack Welch and John A. Byrne, *Jack: Straight from the Gut* (London: Hachette, 2003), p. 12.

Introduction

Better leaders produce better results. Always. This is something that we know for certain and the arguments in support of that proposition are rock solid. And it does not take a Ph.D. in psychology to figure out why. People like to feel appreciated and respected by their boss and when they do, they will give more in return. At least, the majority will do so, and in the world of work you can only ever hope to legislate for the majority. Employee productivity and motivation are always significantly higher in an environment where leadership is strong than when it is not. None of this is ground-breaking stuff of course, the evidence has been heard and the judgment came in a long time ago. There is no reasonable doubt. Case closed. The proof confirming the benefits of effective leadership is so overwhelming that you would be forgiven for thinking that the Impostor Leaders would have no place to hide by now. Unfortunately, reality tells us otherwise.

Everyone has at least one story to tell about a bad boss they had to face at some point in their working life. For an unfortunate few, they could probably write a book on their experience given the severity of what they encountered. I too have come across many harrowing examples over the years: as an employee, manager, and then watching them in action as I consulted for various organizations. But stories alone do not necessarily signify that there is a bad boss problem. It is easy to discount individual experiences as one-offs, or as mentioned, to blame the victim not the aggressor. Thankfully, or should that be unfortunately, there are more than stories to confirm the existence of the Impostor Leaders: just Google 'Research on the effects of bad leadership,' or similar, and see for yourself. Over 300,000 results the last time I checked.

Clearly, a significant number of employees – at all levels and across all industries – remain disillusioned with how they are managed. That is not to say that they are all suffering in the same way, or to the same degree, but many are experiencing a tough time under Impostors. And it is not just employees who are unhappy either. Senior executives frequently bemoan the quality and effectiveness of managers available at more junior ranks. So, a substantial Impostor Leader phenomenon does exist, no matter how much some people might like to pretend otherwise.

Like it or not, Impostors can be found in every organization, on all rungs of the corporate ladder. Sometimes they are perched at the top, where they impact on everyone, or they can be seen skulking further down the chain of command where they cast a long shadow over the daily lives of their direct reports. Despite all that is known about the benefits of effective leadership, Impostors continue to be a far too common feature of organizational life today. Our focus throughout this book will be to see what can be gained from exploring their world. After all, seeing as we are stuck with them, we might as well get some benefit from that fact.

In doing so, an early challenge will be to define more clearly who they are and what they do that is so wrong. That is critical because there are different types of Impostors and obviously not all of them wound to an equal degree: some damage by omission, others by commission. An important first step in this will be to reflect on what Genuine Leadership is all about and based on that discovery to highlight what it is that makes an Impostor. Once they are unmasked so to speak, the spotlight will then shift to their great deception, how they first fool themselves before they get around to deceiving anyone else. From there we will examine how limited they are as leaders because they lack some of the attributes and skills required to lead effectively. At all times, the intent is to contrast the failings of the Impostor Leaders with what effective leaders do, the goal being to help you to think about what you currently do and how well you do it.

Keep it Simple, Stupid

Although leading others is certainly not an easy undertaking, where we can, we will examine the issue in relatively straightforward terms because the hype and complexity surrounding leadership have spiraled out of control in recent decades. Take a quick browse through the business section of any bookstore, online or bricks and mortar, and see just how many ways there are to essentially say the same thing. When it comes to leadership, we sped past overkill quite some time ago and the topic is now swamped in competing concepts, models, and an unbelievable amount of jargon. If leadership is not authentic, it is transformational, or extraordinary. If it is not an art, there are special laws to it, or a secret code that you can somehow magically learn. If the leader is not already within you, then awaken it, or even better, transform into one in a minute. Or how about becoming a revolutionary leader? Apparently, that too is now an option, if you are so inclined.

The subject of leadership is suffering from a severe case of what I like to call the peacock syndrome as it seems that ideas must be fancied up to make them stand out. The bigger and brighter feathers get more attention, or so it would appear. For me, one of the most annoying aspects of this competition to get noticed is how certain commentators depict work leaders as being akin to messiahs who have 'followers' desperately longing to be taken to some organizational promised land. I intensely dislike that image, mainly because it is total nonsense. As far as I am concerned, any leader who thinks of their people as 'followers' does not actually understand leadership in today's workplace.

There are, for sure, exceptional business leaders out there, but they are a minority of a minority. I have been around the block a few times and have met some pretty good leaders along the way, but I have never met anyone that I would 'follow.' Did I respect and admire them? Undoubtedly, I did. Would I have worked my backside off for them? Yes, indeed. And I did so. Would I have gone that extra mile for them? Absolutely, I did on many occasions. But follow them? In a work setting? Sorry, I do not think so. That analogy simply does not work for me, and most managers and employees that I encounter think the same because they are not looking to follow anyone. If anything, they want their bosses to view them as partners, not drones who are willing to line up behind them like lemmings. In attempting to learn from the Impostor Leaders, I think we need to return to earth and get real about some of the leader-follower drivel promoted by some.

During his first presidential campaign, Barack Obama got himself into a little bit of hot water for saying "You know, you can put lipstick on a pig, but it is still a pig,"[1] in response to claims by his Republican opponents that they were the real change agents; the inference being that you can dress things up all you like, but underneath it is still the same. The incident caused quite a stir at the time, yet Obama was spot on with the point he was making. No matter how much you want to fancy something up, it does not change what lies at the core. There is a lesson to be learned from that incident in terms of how we approach leadership. As we move ahead, perhaps it is time to take the lipstick off the leadership pig and return to some basic principles.

Managing and leading (we will get to those distinctions shortly) are undeniably big challenges, and nobody in their right mind would argue otherwise. But the route map for success is to be found, where it has always been, firmly embedded within the sphere of human relations. This should not be forgotten, and it is important not to be swayed by all the gloss and sexy packaging. At the heart of being a great manager or leader lie some fundamental, common-sense principles that guide all human interactions and business activities. These remain the same no matter how much certain people might like to doll them up.

Simplicity is therefore best and where practical and helpful that will be the route taken throughout the book, while bearing in mind Einstein's advice that "everything should be made as simple as possible, but not simpler."[2] When you talk to employees at all levels who are collectively unhappy with their boss, as I frequently do, the majority of that unhappiness can be traced back to basic issues such as people feeling mistreated, not listened to, or excluded from decision making. In other words, normal human wants and needs. In all the time that I have spent working with managers and their teams, I have never heard people complain about their boss because they did not think she was an extraordinary hero, or that he could not soar like an eagle. No, to my mind, employees have realistic expectations of their leaders most of the time. For all of that, many so-called leaders – the Impostors – still do not seem capable of fulfilling them. The focus here will be to examine how and why they fail to master these basics and to learn the lessons.

So, even though much of what will be covered in the pages ahead may not be entirely new to you, do not rubbish it on those grounds alone, or tune out because you cannot find too much fancy plumage sprouting from between the lines. Try to avoid equating lack of glitter with lack of substance. Instead, as you read along, ask not whether you understand the principles of effective leadership explored here – because for the most part you probably already will – but focus on whether you, unlike an Impostor Leader, consistently apply them to the best of your ability each day. Ask not what you think of yourself as a leader, but how others view you. Constantly think about whether those around you consider you to be a Genuine Leader or an Impostor.

Notes

1 '"Lipstick on a Pig": Attack on Palin or Common Line?' CNN, online edition. September 10, 2008. https://edition.cnn.com/2008/POLITICS/09/10/campaign.lip stick. Accessed August 18, 2020.
2 BrainyQuote. www.brainyquote.com/quotes/quotes/a/alberteins103652.html. Accessed August 18, 2020.

Chapter 1

Leadership in Context

"My boss makes me sick." How many times have we all heard someone say this, or similar? Sometimes it is simply born out of frustration in the moment and the anger quickly passes; on other occasions though the relationship with the boss can deteriorate to such an extent that is potentially damaging to the employee's health. It should be obvious that working for a poor leader can be frustrating, or worse still, painful for those at the receiving end of their ineptitude. Now, an increasing body of research suggests that prolonged exposure to them can lead to negative and lasting health impacts.[1] And the findings of such research indicate that the harmful effects of poor leadership may be cumulative – the risk goes up the longer an employee works for the bad boss. We put health warnings on cigarette packs these days, maybe it is time to start labelling certain bosses.

Okay, on the face of it, damaging health effects might seem like an extreme consequence resulting from bad leadership and it is easy to discount such claims as scaremongering. In fact, when I mentioned that concern to a group of executives on a leadership program recently, I was virtually laughed out of the room. Many of those in attendance were quick to pooh-pooh the assertion that bad leaders can measurably impact an individual's health: damn lies and statistics was the thrust of the argument against any research producing such findings. I find it funny how quickly some people will discount solid evidence or shoot the messenger just because it runs contrary to what they want to believe. Anyway, like it or not, the evidence against the Impostor Leaders is certainly there to see, for those willing to see it, and the common theme in all the research I have reviewed is that there is a significant price to pay – emotional and otherwise – for bad leadership, which often goes unnoticed or, worse still, is swept under the carpet. Impostors are not cost-neutral and although those costs may be intangible, or at times hard to quantify, they are far from inconsequential when you factor in the aggregated expenses of reduced engagement, lost productivity, higher employee turnover (particularly the talented ones), increased recruitment costs and so on. If only more organizations would bother to measure those downsides.

Although the negative consequences of bad bosses are starting to get a lot more attention these days, the scale of the problem remains very difficult to gauge and defining the proportion of leaders out there who actually deserve the Impostor tag is relatively unresearched, although that too is changing. Truth be known, the full extent of the Impostor Leader problem probably can never be fully measured. In the first place, what constitutes one is open to some debate; my worst nightmare may well be an acceptable leader to you, and vice versa. It is all very subjective indeed and based as much on opinion as it is on anything else. Add to this the fact that the number of these Impostors hanging around depends on a host of factors including organization culture, industry-type, and indeed quality of employees. Their precise number is not really the core issue anyway, for even one Impostor in an organization is one too many. In my experience, every organization has at least one.

The intention throughout this book is not to get too hung up on trying to measure the scale and costs associated with Impostor Leaders, other than to emphasize that there is plenty of solid research which shows that there are more of them around than many would like to admit; and that they are causing untold psychological and financial damage. Our primary focus will be on what practical leadership lessons might be drawn from shedding light on the common and recurrent misdemeanors of these Impostors.

In doing so, it is impossible to make sense of the issue in isolation. Context is everything as they say, so a little bit of preparation is required to build a solid foundation for what comes later. Leaders, both good and bad, operate in the work environment so it is important to touch on some basic questions about the nature of work itself, the role of leaders, and what employees expect from them in order to provide meaningful background for what lies ahead. The purpose of this chapter is to explore the answers to these important questions to set the scene for exposing the Impostor Leaders.

A Basic Equation of Work

As good a place as any to begin the journey of exploration about Impostors is to consider the nature of work in organizations. After all, that is where leaders do their thing, so it is important to broadly understand what happens in any organization, of any size, in any field.

Every organization is a complex ecosystem of interlocking factors and the primary role of managers is to pull all these strands together so that goals and objectives can be achieved. Applying a non-theoretical interpretation, work is essentially about balancing three interdependent and sometimes competing, dimensions: *Performance*, *Process*, and *People* (Figure 1.1).

- *Performance* relates to what the organization is trying to achieve and includes concerns such as: purpose, goals, strategy, targets, financial

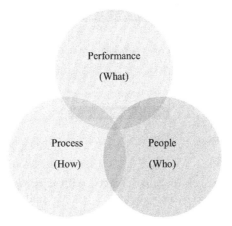

Figure 1.1 Key Dimensions of Work: Performance, Process, and People

results, and other desired outcomes. For any commercial enterprise, these targets will include satisfying customers, achieving profitability, and making an acceptable return on investment. In non-profits, this will vary, but you get the picture. Results matter in any organization.

- *Process* refers to how those results are achieved, and involves defining roles and responsibilities, planning, executing, managing key functions such as marketing and finance and maintaining standards to name but some considerations. The goal in any organization should be to implement the best systems and create the right conditions to deliver the highest possible levels of *productivity*, *efficiency*, and *quality*.
- *People* relates to the employees who do the work every day and incorporates issues such as organization culture, teamwork, individual and team behaviors and applying effective leadership styles. Leaders must get the best from employees by ensuring their *commitment, competence*, and *motivation*.

There are more substantial models around that seek to define the nature of work, but in a nutshell these three dimensions capture what it is all about. The interrelationship between these dimensions can be nicely summarized by a basic equation (Figure 1.2). Maybe this equation does not have as many bells and whistles on it as some of the other frameworks you might come across, but it is just as effective in making the point. Every person holding a position of authority in any organization, regardless of seniority, has some responsibility for balancing this equation although how they do that in practice will naturally depend upon the level involved.

For instance, senior managers may well focus more on setting strategy and defining targets (performance) but they cannot ignore either process or people.

Figure 1.2 A Basic Equation of Work

Equally, middle managers may be charged with execution (process) but in doing so they must engage their employees (people) and they cannot be truly effective without an understanding of what the overall strategy (performance) is. Front line supervisors may devote a lot of attention on the ground to getting the job done to the right standard (process) and this will only be achieved if they bring the best out of their teams (people). Still, even at this level, broad familiarity with the big picture (performance) is also vital.

Success in any organization is therefore largely determined by how well these three dimensions are entwined every day. It is certainly a constant juggling act. This leads us to a related question as to how best to keep all the balls in the air. Is it management or leadership which delivers the greatest results? In laying the foundation for any analysis of Impostor Leaders, this is a critical point for us to investigate.

A Tiresome Debate

Many moons ago, back in November 1988 to be precise, three hundred students from the Hart House Debating Club at the University of Toronto debated the interesting resolution that 'There is nothing not worth talking about,'[2] and managed to keep going at it for a very impressive 388 hours and 15 minutes. Having set a record for the longest running debate ever, a broken tape destroyed the evidence before it could be sent to the *Guinness Book of World Records* for verification. Oh dear, some debates do prove fruitless in the end.

The ongoing debate about the relative importance of the management and leadership functions in organizations can also seem a bit pointless at times. It is not that such issues are unimportant, obviously they are very relevant, but in my experience debating the merits of each tends to throw up as many questions as answers. Significant time and energy are often wasted addressing somewhat abstract concerns like, are management and leadership complementary or mutually exclusive? Can a manager be a leader or a leader a manager? Is leadership a function of management, or the other way around? In fact, I have found that once you get a group of executives going on questions such as these it is hard to get them to stop. Even harder to achieve consensus or to come to any meaningful conclusions.

At the same time, thinking about this inter-relationship is essential because it is impossible at a later stage to point a finger at those who fail the leadership challenge, if what they are supposed to do has not been clearly defined in the first place. It would be unfair and more importantly far too subjective to throw accusations around about Impostors without having some solid evidence to back up that claim: innocent until proven guilty and all that. Yet, finding useful answers to the management–leadership conundrum can prove beyond frustrating and there is no shortage of opinions as to how they relate to one another, with plenty of nice little one-liners to go around like:

- "Management is doing things right; leadership is doing the right things." – Peter Drucker[3]
- "Management is efficiency in climbing the ladder of success; Leadership determines whether the ladder is leaning against the right wall." – Stephen Covey[4]
- "Leadership is the act of accomplishing more than the science of Management says is possible." – General Colin Powell[5]
- "The manager asks how and when; the leader asks what and why." – Warren Bennis[6]

This is all great stuff for certain, but not necessarily very helpful as a practical guide to understanding how leadership and management complement one and other. Catchy and memorable sound bites like these undoubtedly have their place, but they do not really tell us, in any meaningful way at least, how the two roles interrelate in organizations every day in terms of balancing our three dimensions of work. Many believe that leadership is simply a sub-function of management. Others promote the view that it is the reverse. Some argue that the manager-leader roles are essentially one and the same thing. More counter that it is only possible to be one or the other, but not both. It can all get very confusing and indeed exasperating at times.

Here is a good example of how this uncertainty plays out in real life. Hoping to gather the opinions of experienced professionals on this great debate, I conducted a comprehensive online survey of Executive MBA participants some years back. Over 220 of them participated in the study and these mid-career managers represented a broad mix of nationalities and industry fields. When asked whether they believed that leadership and management were essentially the same thing, most of respondents unsurprisingly disagreed (see Table 1.1).

There is a general acceptance that there are differences between leadership and management; this is far from a new or even remotely startling revelation. However, it is when you begin to dig a bit deeper to find out what those differences might be that the real fun starts as the remaining series of results from the survey show in Table 1.2.

Table 1.1 Survey Response 1

Leadership and Management are essentially the same thing. There is too much hype about leadership.

Agree strongly	Agree somewhat	Neither agree nor disagree	Disagree somewhat	Disagree strongly
1%	9%	4%	50%	36%

Table 1.2 Survey Response 2

Leadership is just one of the many skills a successful manager must possess.

Agree strongly	Agree somewhat	Neither agree nor disagree	Disagree somewhat	Disagree strongly
35%	40%	7%	13%	5%

Here in Table 1.2, the commonly held view touched upon earlier that leadership is simply one of the many skills that a manager must possess came to the fore. The popular opinion among this group of MBA executives was that being a leader is something to be done as part of the wider management role, rather than a term which defines an individual. Yet, a quarter of the respondents were not so sure about that to some extent. In a related question, the levels of confusion rose even further (Table 1.3).

These responses in Table 1.3 somewhat contradicted their previous answers, as they signify that leadership is seen as more than a set of skills. The overwhelming majority of the respondents felt that there was some separation between the roles and in seeking to define what those differences might be in the context of the three dimensions of work, the results were as shown in Table 1.4.

Table 1.3 Survey Response 3

A leader can be a manager, but a manager is not necessarily a leader.

Agree strongly	Agree somewhat	Neither agree nor disagree	Disagree somewhat	Disagree strongly
60%	28%	4%	6%	2%

Table 1.4 Survey Response 4

Management focuses on processes and performance. Leadership focuses on people.

Agree strongly	Agree somewhat	Neither agree nor disagree	Disagree somewhat	Disagree strongly
20%	40%	12%	20%	8%

According to Table 1.4, the bulk of participants in the survey considered the differences between leadership and management as relating to the 'hard' and 'soft' aspects of work; or as has been said to me more than a few times over the years, leadership focuses on the 'pink and fluffy' stuff, but management is about getting things done. This again is not an unusual finding. Many managers continue to see the ability to lead as a 'nice to have' but the capacity to manage as a must. At the same time, a not insignificant 40% were against that viewpoint. A linked question about what leaders and managers do further highlighted the ambiguity (Table 1.5).

Here in Table 1.5, about 40% of respondents essentially viewed leaders as thinkers and managers are doers. For them, leaders were seen to be concerned with defining vision and strategy whereas execution was down to managers. However, about the same number disagreed with that opinion. A fair few sat on the fence and, to be honest, that is probably no great surprise. As the debate drags on and the further you delve into it, little clarity emerges and it all becomes a bit mind-numbing. There are more important things to worry about in life right now, like global pandemics for one. Obviously, it got too much for one of the executives who seemed to hit the wall about half-way through the survey, leaving the following comment instead:

> Sorry, I don't have the time (or is it the interest) to get through this. Will come back later to finish, maybe. Actually, this is all way too complicated anyway. Here is the real difference between leadership and management:
>
> • When Noah heard the weather forecast, he ordered the building of the ark. That was Leadership.
> • When he looked around and said, "Make sure the elephants don't see what the rabbits are up to." That was Management.
>
> Simple really.

I had seen that joke plenty of times before, but it still made me chuckle. He or she never did come back and finish off the survey, but who can blame them for that. In any case, these snapshots from the survey of MBA Executives simply confirm what is already well known: confusion rages when the

Table 1.5 Survey Response 5

Leaders focus on the 'big picture,' but ultimately it is the managers who make it a reality.

Agree strongly	Agree somewhat	Neither agree nor disagree	Disagree somewhat	Disagree strongly
6%	36%	18%	27%	13%

subject of management versus leadership comes up. Among any group of experienced managers, there is always a general acceptance that the two functions are distinctive, yet interdependent, but the precise nature of the relationship between them is difficult to describe and is as much a matter of personal perspective as anything else. It is hard to know where management begins and leadership ends.

Is it a Bird? Is it a Plane ...? No, it is a Manaleader

Maybe the debate is therefore best avoided, not simply as a convenient way of bypassing a thorny issue but perhaps it is less important whether we call it management or leadership, and infinitely more interesting what actually happens or should happen in practice. Out there in the real world, there are plenty of managers who are great leaders, others who are less so and then, as we shall see, there are the Impostors. I have also had the honor of meeting individuals with snappy titles such as 'leadership fellows' or 'global leaders' some of whom would not recognize real leadership if it walked up and bit them on the rear-end. So, whether someone calls him or herself a manager or a leader, the specific title they hold is probably irrelevant. Terminology is not really the issue although at times it has become the focus of the debate.

What matters most in daily business life is how those who hold positions of authority at any organizational level think, act, and behave on a consistent basis. To succeed they must be able to balance our three dimensions of work; unless all elements of our earlier work equation are addressed, the desired results cannot be achieved. To do that requires them to both manage and lead and to have the ability to do so continuously to a high standard. You might even say they need to be 'Manaleaders,' for the roles are inseparably intertwined. It is not the case that some individuals serve as leaders in an organization, whereas others act as managers. That is simply impractical. Yes, at times, 'leading' may well take precedence such as when setting overall direction for the business, or when motivating and inspiring employees but process always needs to be 'managed' to deliver the expected levels of performance. Leading and managing are essentially two sides to the one coin and cannot or should not be considered independently.

Manaleaders would therefore be a better title to use today in organizations, as it more closely reflects what is really required. It is a far more accurate description of what is necessary than either the term manager or leader. But, the leadership field has way too much jargon already without adding to it, so we will stick with the term leader for the remainder of this book, although we will mean it strictly in the sense of a Manaleader: someone with the ability to both lead and manage.

Real leaders must therefore be multi-talented individuals capable of fulfilling the needs of both the leadership and management functions. Only the most versatile candidates can come close to harmonizing these conflicting roles. They do not have to be supermen or superwomen, extraordinary heroes, or corporate champions but they must be a cut above the rest and success is as much about how they think as it is about what they do.

It is the sheer depth and breadth of talents required to make it as a leader that exposes individual weaknesses because it is naturally hard for any one person to have all that it takes to be strong at both managing and leading. So, the best leaders are obviously special individuals, nonetheless, they are born on Earth not Krypton; or at least they leave the red tights and cape at home every morning. Becoming a master of all that is required to successfully lead is undoubtedly a major challenge and an inability to do so, as will become clear, is one of the major contributing factors to why there are so many Impostor Leaders around.

What Employees Want

No preparation for an investigation of Impostor Leaders could ever be fully complete without making some reference to those at the receiving end of leadership. After all, one of the true barometers of leadership effectiveness is the quality of the relationships that exist between a leader and her team. Research, and indeed basic common sense, tells us that the leader-employee relationship is not an insignificant one, so understanding what employees look for in their leaders will be helpful in later defining what makes one an Impostor.

When you consider that your boss directly influences the pattern of your life for over two thousand hours in any given year, that emphasizes how significant that relationship is. At least you get to choose your partner, not so your boss in most cases. What matters to employees about this important relationship? What do they look for in their leaders? Do they want to be led or managed? Daily, do people really care, or even think about such intangible concerns? When asked whether they believed that their own direct reports were focused on the issue, our MBA Executives were quite divided in their responses (Table 1.6).

Fifty percent felt that yes, their employees do want to be led not managed, but a quarter disagreed with this and the remaining 25% not sure either way.

Certainly, no sane employee jumps out of bed first thing in the morning and, as they struggle blindly towards the shower, thinks, "Right, I really

Table 1.6 Survey Response 6

Today, people at work do not want to be managed; they want to be led.				
Agree strongly	Agree somewhat	Neither agree nor disagree	Disagree somewhat	Disagree strongly
13%	37%	25%	18%	7%

hope I am going to be led, not managed, today." More likely their focus is elsewhere at that point. But, without reflecting on it too much, people do know that they want to be treated in a certain way and just being 'managed' is not going to fulfil those needs. Employees want to feel valued, respected, and they expect to have a meaningful relationship with their boss, one that is based on openness and trust. That requires leadership. When you dig a bit deeper into what it is that employees expect from their leaders, this desire to be led and not just managed becomes even clearer.

When asked what mattered most personally to them about their immediate boss back at work, the ten most popular expectations of their leaders from the MBA executives, in order of importance, were:

1   Visionary.
2   Good communicator.
3   Good motivator.
4   Charismatic.
5   Inspirational.
6   Determined.
7   Results-/success-driven.
8   Competent.
9   Honesty.
10   Compassionate/understanding.

By means of contrast, the MBA participants were later asked to think of a poor leader they had encountered in the past and to identify the things that this individual did that wound them up. The top ten gripes identified were:

1   Not involving them in decision-making.
2   Micromanaging them.
3   Disrespecting them.
4   Not providing freedom/autonomy.
5   Not giving constructive feedback.
6   Not recognizing effort.
7   Not communicating effectively.
8   Not having, or communicating, an overall vision.
9   Creating negativity or poor team spirit.
10   Ineffective performance/failure to get things done.

There are clearly close linkages between the gripe list and the positive things that the MBA executives looked for in their leaders. Having repeated this exercise many times with groups of both managers and employees over the years, I have noticed that the lists produced are always quite comparable, regardless of what group or level is involved. On all occasions, a repetitive pattern emerges in the responses. What people expect from, or dislike in their leaders, is based upon normal human aspirations to feel appreciated and respected. This is hardly rocket science yet delivering on those expectations is another matter entirely and as we will highlight is often beyond the capabilities of the Impostor Leaders.

What really matters is that when examined closely most of the top-ranked expectations on both lists relate to the people element of our three dimensions of work. This tells us something that is perhaps obvious but no less interesting because of that about what employees are looking for. They are less concerned with how well their leaders can strategize, plan, organize the workload or manage finance; what they care more about are qualities reflective of basic human needs.

Employees want to work for sincere people who can inspire and motivate them, but nowhere have I ever seen them express the desire to 'follow' someone else. As said earlier, the notion of following their leader does not figure in the thinking of most of the people that I encounter. They do, however, want their leader to treat them as a partner and they expect to be dealt with fairly, to be able to respect those who lead them and in turn to feel respected by them. That said, people are not solely content to work for a leader who, although treated them very well, achieved little or lacked competence. Seeing results is important to most employees too.

So, even though employees may not analyze what they want from their bosses in an overtly conscious way, first and foremost, what they are looking for is to work for someone who has good leadership skills, but they also expect their boss to have good management skills as well. It could be said that employees prefer working alongside Manaleaders.

Planets Apart

Finally, in setting the scene for any investigation of Impostor Leaders, it is important to be fair and balanced towards leaders too because they do make easy targets for criticism and it is hard for them to win sometimes. When it comes to the blame game, they are like sitting ducks, the proverbial fish in a barrel you might even say. All leaders face common challenges that must be accounted for when later defining what it is that makes an Impostor.

One of those challenges which every leader must deal with is that, in all organizations, there is always a small percentage of employees who dislike their boss simply because they are the boss. For this minority – those few habitual moaners that infest the world of work – it does not really matter who is in the hot seat because whinging about their leader is almost a vocation. Regardless of who is in charge certain employees will find a reason to criticize. These victims are usually best ignored and preferably shipped out at the earliest opportunity. In all workplaces too, there are frequently a few underperformers who will test the patience of even the best of leaders. Any of our later decisions about what constitutes an Impostor will most certainly not be based on the whims of the disgruntled few, nor will they be informed by the opinions of negative employees.

On that subject of moaning about the boss, everyone does it now and again. It is simply part and parcel of work life. It is healthy in some respects – and normal when infrequent and mild in nature. But, on the odd occasions when you do it try not to repeat the mistake made by a girl named Lindsay who decided to mouth off about her boss on Facebook one evening after work. The incident was once reported on the social news website Digg under the headline: "Why You Shouldn't Have Your Boss on Facebook."[7] One evening, Lindsay posted the following tirade (expletives deleted) against her boss, a man named Brian:

> OMG I hate my job!! My boss is a total pervvy ****, always making me do **** stuff just to **** me off.

Shortly later, her boss, Brian, replied:

> Hi Lindsay, I guess you forgot about adding me on here? Firstly, don't flatter yourself. Secondly, you've worked here 5 months and didn't work out that I'm gay? Thirdly, that **** stuff is called your 'job,' you know what I pay you to do. But the fact that you seem to be able to **** up the simplest of tasks might contribute to how you feel about it. And lastly, you also seem to have forgotten that you have two weeks remaining on your 6-month trial period. Don't bother coming in tomorrow. I'll pop your P45 in the post and you can come in whenever you like to pick up any stuff you've left here. And yes, I'm serious.

Classic! But now back to more important matters.

Thankfully, most employees are – to a greater or lesser degree – positive individuals who are prepared to be supportive of their leaders when that support is earned and deserved. Yet, even in relation to this positive major-ity, leaders still must walk a tightrope since we are talking about work here after all. No matter how 'into' their job someone is, it is still only work, other aspects of life are equally if not far more important for most people. Sometimes, employees can simply be unhappy with what is happening in their lives or with work generally and they can project that unhappiness onto the boss. Regardless of how good the leader is, it is impossible to keep all the people happy all the time. In defining Impostor Leaders, we will also keep this important point in mind.

Perhaps the greatest challenge for all leaders arises because employees tend to view work life from a completely different perspective than they do. There are two sides to every story, as they say. Sometimes employee expec-tations of their leaders can be unrealistic, or on other occasions, what is within the power of their leader to deliver may be constrained by factors unknown to employees such as financial constraints or pressures from above. Leaders can also be under tremendous stress from above to achieve what is expected of them and this can negatively influence their behavior from time to time. Yet, employees rarely understand or allow for that and, over the years, I have been constantly amazed at just how different leader and employee perceptions can be. Undoubtedly, these opposing perspectives can lead to some employees having a negative view of their leader, and this may not necessarily be down to any real failing on that leader's behalf. This too must be factored in when describing Impostor Leaders.

Considering all of this, the definitions of Impostor Leaders that we will begin to address in the next chapter have been strongly influenced by these important considerations. Impostors are not those who fail to keep a few grumblers happy; a couple of dissatisfied employees does not the Impostor Leader make. Nor are they leaders who do not meet all the expectations of their employees all the time. That is clearly an impossible task. They are also not those who get things wrong occasionally, or who are forced to take difficult decisions due to factors which employees do not understand. No, Impostor Leaders are individuals who continually underperform and display repetitive patterns of destructive behaviors, mild or otherwise.

At a conservative estimate, over the past twenty-five plus years, I have consulted for over 500 companies, small and large, across many different fields and in many different countries, so I have seen a thing or two when it comes to how people are led. The categories of Impostors defined in the coming chapters are based on failings that I have regularly, and more crucially, repeatedly seen in ineffective leaders over the years. These descriptions have also been informed by the continuous feedback that I have received from literally thousands of positive managers and employees that I have interacted with who felt disheartened and disgruntled with the performance of their leaders.

Summary

Reflecting upon the nature of work, the role of leaders and what employees expect of them provides a solid foundation for analyzing the world of the Impostor Leaders. It demonstrates that being an effective 'leader' today actually requires individuals who have the capacity to both manage and lead, which in turn means having a broad range of personal characteristics and competences. At times leaders can take flak from all sides, from superiors and subordinates, so they must continuously respond to the many, often contradictory, demands and challenges they face. As a result, leading others is a far more expansive undertaking than is often fully appreciated, and it is one which only the very best individuals can ever hope to do consistently well.

Unfortunately, in many organizations, individuals are still appointed into leadership positions or retain existing posts despite clearly lacking the depth and breadth of characteristics and skills necessary to manage and lead effectively. It should not come as too much of a surprise therefore to find that there are a fair few Impostor Leaders about.

The following chapter begins the process of defining who the Impostors are by first exploring what it is that all leaders should do in order to be successful and, based on that, presenting a framework for separating real leaders from the Impostors.

Notes

1 Anna Nyberg, *The Impact of Managerial Leadership on Stress and Health among Employees* (Stockholm: Karolinska Institutet, 2009).
2 'Fighting Words.' University of Toronto. https://magazine.utoronto.ca/campus/history/history-of-debating-at-u-of-t-hart-house. Accessed August 18, 2020.
3 BrainyQuote. www.brainyquote.com/quotes/peter_drucker_131069. Accessed August 18, 2020.
4 BrainyQuote. www.brainyquote.com/authors/stephen-covey-quotes. Accessed August 18, 2020.
5 '13 Rules of Leadership by Colin Powell.' Center for Executive Excellence. September 18, 2013. https://executiveexcellence.com/13-rules-leadership-colin-powell. Accessed August 18, 2020.
6 BrainyQuote. www.brainyquote.com/authors/warren-bennis-quotes. Accessed August 18, 2020.
7 'Woman "Sacked" after Abusing Boss on Facebook.' *The Telegraph*, online edition. August 14, 2009. www.telegraph.co.uk/technology/facebook/6027302/Woman-sacked-after-abusing-boss-on-Facebook.html. Accessed August 18, 2020.

Chapter 2

The Many Faces of Leadership

Ayumu seemed to really enjoy his moment in the limelight. Well, it would appear so, if the big smile he had on his face after the event was anything to go by. In a televised head-to-head contest that involved remembering the position of numbers on a screen, the seven-year-old male chimp raised in captivity did three times better than the reigning world memory champion at that time. This was not a minor achievement for Ayumu when you consider that one of his opponent's talents was memorizing the sequence of a shuffled pack of cards in under thirty seconds![1]

In the test, digits were shown on the screen for just one-fifth of a second and then hidden by white squares. The two contestants had to touch the squares in the order that the numbers had appeared. Ayumu got it right an amazing 90% of the time, whereas the poor old human scored a comparatively miserable 33%. "I'm the chimpion!" was the popular tabloid headline after the contest, accompanied by a photo of a beaming but suspiciously smug-looking Ayumu holding a banana.

It is well known that chimpanzees share a large proportion of their DNA with us. They are undoubtedly our close relatives and, in some ways, manage to outdo us. Yet, despite the shared genes and his penchant for number games, it is highly improbable that Ayumu would be mistaken for a human in a police line-up because similar does not necessarily mean the same. This analogy also applies in the leadership arena. Although all leaders do of course share a similar genetic make-up, they are most definitely not all the same. Some truly excel in the role, while others simply fail to cut it. Naturally, you cannot tell the good from bad just by looking at them, but spend time in the company of each and their talents and shortcomings as leaders will quickly emerge. In the leadership line-up, there are real leaders and then there are the Impostors.

Separating the wheat from the chaff when it comes to leaders is no easy task, though, as clearly none of them get it all right, or indeed all wrong. Every leader's performance is subject to peaks and troughs of some kind and we all have our good and bad days; some more bad than good, unfortunately, as we will see. But when judged over the long term, I have seen how certain leaders continually outperform others, sometimes by a significant margin. To explore this gap and to begin defining who the Impostor Leaders are, some sort of benchmark that helps to make sense of the diversity found in leader performance would be useful. Such a framework is not just useful but essential to allow for a more objective definition of the Impostors.

This chapter provides one in the form of the Leadership Wheel – a new conceptual framework I have developed that distinguishes good leaders from bad. It will help to put names to the many faces of leadership found in organizations, albeit with an acknowledgement that no one model can ever hope to account for every single type of leadership behavior seen. The Wheel will however assist in identifying the different types of Impostor Leaders based on a comparison against what effective leaders do.

Engage to Achieve – The Missing Link

People are not mass-produced goods and they cannot be pigeonholed or slotted into neat little categories just because we would like them to. Each of us is unique, so no two people will, or indeed should, think and act alike all the time. This principle is just as applicable when it comes to leaders. Individuality aside, though, what leaders do and how they do it can be far more uniform and predictable than they might like to think, particularly when judged over a sustained period. It is possible to start distinguishing leader performance by how well they consistently – and that word is crucial here – combine the leadership and management roles.

The most effective leaders you will encounter are those that make a positive and lasting impact on organizational life, appropriate to their level on the corporate ladder. They are the Manaleaders we talked about. They are so, because more times than not, they can find the right balance between our three dimensions of work – People, Process and Performance. In other words, they continually do two things well (Table 2.1).

The best leaders that I have seen can engage their people to achieve outstanding results, and they can do it consistently over the long term. They both lead and manage well. Good for people, in the sense that their employees feel involved with and valued by them, the very best leaders are also good for process and performance because they produce above-the-norm results. When you

Table 2.1 Balancing the Three Dimensions of Work

Engage	Engaging People to ensure their commitment, competence, and motivation.	The 'Leading' part
Achieve	Harnessing that engagement by focusing on *Process* to ensure productivity, efficiency, and quality in order to achieve the *Performance* and results required.	The 'Managing' part

probe what lies behind their success, you invariably find that all great leaders have a strongly held belief – which goes beyond lip service – that it is through increased employee engagement that organizational goals and objectives are achieved. The Impostors are who they are in part because they miss or indeed intentionally overlook this vital link. How well any leader gets to grips with balancing the engage to achieve dynamic will be a major determinant in sorting the good from bad, so it is helpful to spend some time reflecting on what employee engagement is all about and what needs to be done to realize it.

What is Employee Engagement?

While employee engagement might well be a current 'in' term, it is hardly a totally new concept. There is a bit of the lipstick and pig syndrome going on here too, I fear. Concerns about issues such as motivation, empowerment, employee satisfaction and productivity, and employee value propositions have been around a fair while, and engagement is essentially an umbrella term which pulls all these strands together. But engaging employees is not just about generating high satisfaction levels. It moves beyond that worthy aim because it is focused on translating that contentment into higher productivity and performance to maximize the contribution that employees make, individually and collectively, to organizational results.

Hoping to develop truly engaged employees essentially means paying attention to anything that can positively or negatively impact on individual and collective performance, with the consequence that the factors influencing employee engagement are many and varied. The 'engage to achieve' link clearly is not that hard to grasp – few argue against it in principle – but it is far from easy to attain in practice. In the words of Richard Branson: "Loyal employees in a company create loyal customers, who in turn create happy shareholders. The process sounds easy, but it is not, and it has defeated some of the bigger organizations of the twentieth century."[2]

Now whatever your views on Mr Branson, it is hard to make a counter-argument about the role of people in delivering success. Yet, many international studies of engagement continually highlight that most employees are either under engaged or actively undermining their work. There are many reasons behind this, but the research also indicates that poor leadership is always a significant contributing factor. With such a large proportion of people giving less than they could, employees remain an under-tapped resource in most organizations, and failure to engage ultimately means failure to achieve the best results possible.

Despite the difficulties in trying to optimize employee engagement, it is certainly worth the effort because an engaged employee can make a massive difference to the organization they work for and for the customers they interact with. Here is a very simple example that I experienced which proves the point:

Recently, I had an experience while travelling which really drove home the importance of having engaged employees, no matter what the industry involved. Having travelled for almost twelve hours, suffering the usual chaos that is air travel today, I arrived at my destination in less than good humor. After checking in at the hotel, I went to my room and began unpacking, only to realize that I had forgotten to pack any shirts – never a good idea when making a major presentation the following day.

I raced to the nearest department store I could find only to be greeted by a 'jobsworth' security employee at the door who informed me that as the store was closing shortly, I could not go to the men's department on the third floor, under any circumstances. Suppressing the urge to throttle him, I turned on my heels to see if I could find another option, when a second store employee called after me. He said that he could clearly see that I was looking for something urgent and if I promised to be quick, he would help me find it and promptly escorted me to the third floor. Unfortunately, there was not anything in my size or even close to it, but this young man was unperturbed and explained that they had another branch relatively nearby in a taxi which was late opening. He offered to call and see if they had what I was looking for – which they did – and he requested that they put it on hold.

Now this is a very minor incident in the greater scheme of things, but it highlights the fact that when employees are engaged, they see beyond rules and regulations, or their own needs, to focus on the customer. They deliver more and this in turn helps the organization to realize its objectives. This rule applies, no matter what the industry or organization involved. The best leaders inherently get this fact and that is why they work so hard to really engage their people to the highest level possible. They fundamentally recognize that progress towards organizational goals and targets is always faster and smoother when employees are truly engaged.

Drivers of Engagement

But what can be practically done to better engage employees? This is perhaps one of the most common questions that I get asked. In fact, it has arisen in one shape or form on every leadership course that I have ever delivered. So much so that it has become something of a personal quest to try and define what the key drivers of engagement are. For many years, when working with groups of employees I always question them as to what really engages them and unsurprisingly their responses are broadly the same. A sample of the type of comments that come up are shown:

• "Having a good relationship with my boss."
• "Interesting and challenging work."

- "Feeling appreciated."
- "Getting results and moving forward."
- "Mentoring and encouragement, trust."
- "Provoking change and seeing it happen."
- "Doing good through intellectually stimulating work."
- "Being able to achieve/contribute to something meaningful."
- "Self-achievement."
- "Believing in what I do."
- "Involvement and inspiration."
- "Empowerment, trust, team spirit."
- "Striving for excellence."
- "Powerful common mission, congruent rules and instructions, fun and cooperation."
- "Reward for creativity and innovation."

What is so interesting here is that the comments from diverse groups of employees are always comparable. They generally relate to people feeling appreciated for what they do, getting some sense of meaning or challenge out of their job and, always top of the list, having a good relationship with their boss. Note that there is no mention here either of wanting to follow their leader. Equally, when interacting with leaders, or consulting in-company, I have also constantly been on the lookout for what it is that the better leaders and organizations do to maximize engagement.

There is no magic pill of course, but from comparing best practices seen in companies where engagement is high, I have come up with a list of twelve factors that all leaders need to be concerned with to really engage their people.

- **Leadership.** It should be obvious that no one thing will, on its own, fully address the engagement issue, but I am convinced that when leadership is strong, engagement levels tend to be higher, so Genuine Leadership is certainly the most critical first step. As well as their own capabilities, to really engage their people, leaders also need to consider the remaining drivers.
- **Ethos.** Ethos, or culture, call it what you will, is intangible at the best of times but it has a major impact on the feel or climate in any organization. While there is no 'right' ethos, there are certain environments that build engagement, whereas others have the opposite effect. I have seen how the best leaders play an important role in building a culture which draws employees in rather than pushes them away.
- **Mix.** What I mean here is the make-up of teams and all leaders need to pay close attention to how they recruit people into existing teams. Employees do not necessarily all have to like each other, nor will they, but there must be a general 'fit' between team members, otherwise it is

hard to engage them because who wants to work alongside a bunch of people with whom you have little or nothing in common.

- **Direction.** In this context means ensuring that employees understand both aspirations and expectations. Aspirations relate to the big picture and, as a basic building block of engagement, leaders need to help employees fully understand where the organization is going and how they can contribute to that. Clarity is also required as to what is expected of employees, as nothing will destroy engagement faster than conflicting directions or shifting roles and responsibilities.
- **Talents.** This factor contributes to engagement in several ways. First, most employees that I have met want to build their talents at work, so to increase engagement, leaders need to ensure that there are relevant and regular opportunities for personal development. Equally, all employees should be similarly competent at what they are expected to do. If not, others in the team must take up the slack and this creates resentment, or (worse still) conflict, which can chip away at engagement.
- **Spirit.** It goes without saying that team spirit and levels of cooperation are both a driver of engagement and a reflection of it. When people work well together, they build bonds and trust increases. This in turn improves general engagement levels because most people prefer to work in collaborative environments.
- **Discipline.** Sounds like an old-fashioned concept but controlling how individuals behave within teams is critical to engagement. If certain team members can step out of line without consequence, this serves as a de-motivating factor for engaged employees as they question why they should bother. Equally, too much discipline or control within the work environment stifles engagement because people sense a lack of freedom and autonomy.
- **Connection.** There is not much to be said here. Communication builds connections and is therefore key to the levels of engagement seen. Where communication is regular, open, two-way, and more importantly effective, employees tend to be more connected and engaged in my experience.
- **Buzz.** For most employees having a sense of excitement and challenge in their work is also vital to how engaged they feel with the organization. When work feels repetitive or mundane, employees naturally feel less engaged, so leaders need to find ways to introduce a sense of excitement for employees, to create a buzz about the place.
- **Conflict.** The way that conflict is managed can have a major impact on how engaged employees are likely to be. Constructive conflict, which leads to new ideas and better solutions should be encouraged, but well managed, so that employees feel that they can speak their minds or contribute in an appropriate manner. I am a strong believer that destructive conflict, on the other hand, which adds no value should be dealt with

promptly by the leader; a failure to do so will impact engagement levels as most people hate to work in a poisoned atmosphere.

- **Rewards.** In the broadest sense is about people feeling rewarded for the contribution they make. Pay and conditions are of course important elements in this, but it is amazing just how powerful factors like constructive feedback and positive recognition when deserved can be in terms of building engagement.
- **Change.** How change is managed can also impact on the levels of engagement seen. Too little change can result in stagnation which destroys engagement. Yet I have frequently seen how too much of it, or too much meaningless change, can simply frustrate employees and causes them to disengage.

The best leaders, apart from constantly striving to raise their own game in terms of how they engage others, also pay close attention to these factors. They do so because they know that this will not only build engagement levels, but more importantly will in turn lead to greater productivity and ultimately better results. What strikes me about the better leaders that I have met is that they seem to really understand that nothing can ever truly be achieved if employees do not buy into organizational aims and that lifting each individual's level of engagement, even by a small amount, can make a big difference collectively. They really seem to believe in the value of individual contributions. This belief in the inherent value of the individual was nicely summed up by Anita Roddick, founder of The Body Shop, when she once said, "If you think you're too small to have an impact, try going to bed with a mosquito."[3]

The main focus of this book is primarily on individual leader performance but the ability of any leader to positively influence all the key drivers of engagement also plays a major role in determining whether they turn out to be an effective leader or an Impostor.

Introducing the Leadership Wheel

Staying with the 'engage to achieve' concept, it is now possible to begin separating true leaders from Impostors based on how well they cope with this interrelationship. The Leadership Wheel (Figure 2.1) identifies four broad categories of leaders according to their ability to intertwine the leadership (engage) and management (achieve) roles.

I do not intend the Wheel to be viewed as a personality profile of leaders, but it does describe the general types commonly found based on how they consistently perform and behave over the long term.

Where a leader sits on the Wheel most of the time results from their capacity to engage or alienate their people plotted against their propensity to achieve or underachieve when it comes to results. The center of the Wheel shows the four categories of leaders:

- Genuine Leaders.
- Nearly Leaders.
- Deflating Impostors.
- Toxic Impostors.

Keep these four overall categories in mind, as we will be referring to them continuously from now on. The Wheel highlights that there are two groupings of what are deemed positive leaders – *Genuine* and *Nearly* – with two classes of Impostors – *Deflating* and *Toxic* – those who underperform when it comes to engaging employees, achieving results, or indeed both. The inner ring of the wheel (in grey) shows the most common type of leader found in each category, while the outer ring (black) shows the minority, which in the case of the Genuine Leaders, for example, means that Nurturers are the most prevalent whereas Stars are less often seen.

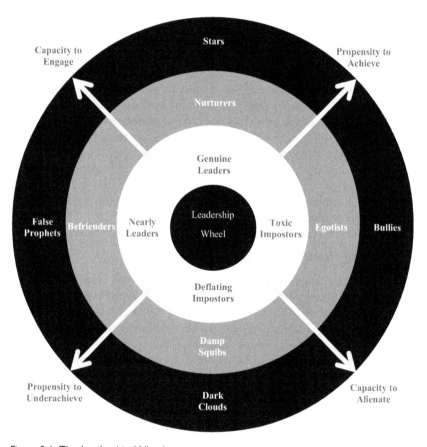

Figure 2.1 The Leadership Wheel

As a bit of fun, and to help provide initial meaning for the Wheel, outside of a work context, where would you slot the following present and past political leaders against the above four categories (ignore the sub-categories for the moment until we explore them a bit)?

- Barack Obama.
- Theresa May.
- Donald Trump.
- Bill Clinton.
- Boris Johnson.
- Tony Blair.
- Angela Merkel.
- Vladimir Putin.

Once you learn more about the categories, you will be quite surprised how quickly you can plot some people against the Wheel, and how others are a bit harder to categorize.

Now, maybe your initial thoughts are that all of this seems suspiciously like pigeonholing to you. These catchy little categories cannot be a realistic portrayal of what goes on in organizations every day when it comes to leadership, can they? Actually, the Wheel works well when you accept some important points that lie behind it:

- All leaders are, of course, individuals; each has his or her own personality and possesses distinctive strengths and weaknesses. Every one of them has the capacity on occasion to rotate between the four categories, to some degree at least. We all have an inner Impostor within us which surfaces from time to time – hence the wheel idea – and leaders can at times show the strengths or weaknesses associated with different categories. That is just normal human frailty in action. But over the long term, when sustained performance is considered, I have seen how leaders tend to spend more of their time in a single category based on how, and how well, they perform. In other words, leaders tend to display the characteristics and behaviors associated with a specific leader-type most of the time.
- The Impostors Leaders do not necessarily 'fail' as such, for outright failure would not be tolerated for very long in any organization today. What they do, though, is consistently underperform in different ways and for different reasons. They are designated Impostors not because of infrequent lapses, instead, they are repeat offenders and frequently display negative behaviors which cause them problems. More of the time than not, they are stuck in Impostor mode.

So, the Leadership Wheel has little to do with individual personality and everything to do with common patterns of behavior and enduring quality of performance. For that reason, it works well because it is reflective of the real world. I have encountered all these leader types many times over the years and as mentioned when you get to know them better, no doubt you will have too. Isolating the most frequently seen types of leaders also helps to define the benefits that Genuine Leaders bring to the table, or the damage that each of the Impostors can cause in organizations which will be helpful as you reflect on your own capabilities as a leader and in making the case why all leaders should seek to aim for Genuine Leadership.

In reading ahead, it is as useful to think about the qualities and behaviors associated with all leader categories and types as it is to focus on any one category. Try to reflect on what talents you share with the positive leaders and the shortcomings you might repeatedly display in common with the Impostors.

A quick snapshot of the four categories is provided here, but the following chapters will take a more detailed look at what they do or do not do that earns them a particular label.

- **Genuine Leaders.** Meet the Manaleaders. Far from perfect or infallible by any means, these leaders do however possess the required talents to lead effectively and they make a concerted effort to apply positive leadership approaches based on the notion that employees are partners, not followers. They focus both on improving their own abilities as a leader and on optimizing the remaining drivers of engagement with the result that they have a high capacity to engage their people and a strong propensity to achieve results. What impresses me about the Genuine Leaders I have met is that they consistently get the leadership–management balance right by focusing on the needs of their employees without taking their eyes off organizational goals; they are relationship-orientated, but results-driven.
- **Nearly Leaders.** These leaders do not achieve the same levels of excellence seen in Genuine Leaders but for the most part their hearts are in the right place. For this reason, it would be wrong to tar them with the Impostor brush even though their performance does not always succeed in getting leadership and management in alignment. I find that they are doing their best to engage their people, but several personal failings prevent them from reaching the highest levels of performance.
- **Deflating Impostors.** These guys are not all bad of course and generally they are not completely malicious characters. But their behaviors, intentionally and otherwise, tend to sap the enthusiasm and passion out of employees over time. I have regularly seen how they fall down on the engagement side not only because of their own poor leadership capabilities but in relation to the other drivers too, like the culture they create or in how they actually reduce the challenge of work life. Ultimately, they are not so good for people, process, or performance

because they create a highly controlled, or at times stifling, working environment which increasingly alienates some or all of those who work for them. This in turn means they have a greater propensity to underachieve in terms of the results they generate.

- **Toxic Impostors.** These leaders are a dangerous bunch and as a result deserve a lot of attention. They can, and do, achieve positive results within the organization but it is in how they do so that creates the problems. Toxic Impostors not only alienate their people but can inflict a fair degree of pain on some of them too, emotionally speaking of course. I have a strong disliking for them. They pay little or no attention either to their own leadership capabilities or to any of the remaining drivers of engagement and as a result they must push their people hard to get the results they want. They are only results driven.

At this stage, it is worth making what may be an obvious point concerning the various types of leaders found in any company. From my interactions across many different industries and organizations, I have noticed that there are many factors at play which determine the mix between positive leaders and Impostors seen. Sometimes, it is the nature of the industry which has a role to play in it. Certain fields, particularly where there is potential for high financial reward, can encourage a specific type of Impostor behavior. It can often be a badge of honor to be an aggressive go-getting browbeater. Think Wall Street here, if in any doubt. Of course, the opposite is true too and other fields can provide a rich environment for different types of Impostors.

National and organization culture too can influence the mix. Some workplaces suffer from 'macho' cultures where there is a belief that only the fittest can survive and prosper, others are more collaborative in nature. Even the type of employees, what they are collectively prepared to accept and how much power they wield can often be an important contributor to how extreme the Impostor problem is. Individuals can also be a factor, some people are drawn to bad leaders, or others lack the capacity to deal with them. The goal in any organization should obviously be to create the conditions that promote positive leadership and discourages *Impostorism*.

The Best Leaders Are Made of the 'Right Stuff'

Optimizing the engage–achieve relationship is evidently not an easy task and represents a real challenge every day. Nor, it must be said, is it possible to get it right all the time, because they are often competing forces. That is why only the most talented individuals can ever hope to get close to that ideal. Lots try, but only some – the Genuine Leaders – get it right more of the time than wrong. What is it though that helps these leaders to outshine their peers? What do they have that is lacking in the Impostors?

In his celebrated book *The Right Stuff*, Tom Wolfe painted a vivid picture of the American military pilots who helped to pioneer the NASA space program.[4] He tells the compelling story about these volunteer test pilots as they participated in early testing and describes how the seven Mercury astronauts were selected and later trained. His book is largely about the heroism of these men and particularly focuses on who they were as people and how they lived by an unspoken set of standards and assumptions which was summed up as having 'the right stuff.' In the book Wolfe himself described these individuals as "that elite who had the capacity to bring tears to men's eyes, the very Brotherhood of the Right Stuff itself."

Clearly, the requirements to succeed as an astronaut differ from those needed to make it as a work leader. Yet, it goes without saying that the best leaders too need something special if they are to succeed and having some form of the right stuff is essential in any leadership context. Although it is hardly revolutionary to promote the idea that people need certain traits and skills to lead effectively, at the same time, when you talk to leaders it is not always as clear regarding which are more important – is it the traits or the skills?

Obviously, there are a range of skills which are critical to leading effectively and only a fool would dispute that fact. All too frequently leadership potential is too narrowly focused on the skills side, but I am convinced that how leaders think and who they are on the inside is far more important. In fact, it is not just my opinion because there is an abundance of research on why leaders fail which shows that issues like self-awareness, mindset, and personal qualities are probably of equal if not more importance than skills as determinants of success.

Most of the flaws seen in underperforming leaders, I find, are related as much to who they are as people, as they do to the skills they may or may not possess. Skills alone, while essential, are of little use if a leader does not have certain personal characteristics and a way of thinking that underpins positive leadership. Therefore, the best leaders are something before they do anything. It is who they are as much as what they do which separates the good from bad. You might say that Genuine Leaders are made of the right stuff (Figure 2.2).

Having the right stuff helps Genuine Leaders to better balance the engage-achieve relationship:

- **How they think.** The high levels of self-awareness I have seen in all Genuine Leaders allows them to play to their strengths and minimize the impact of their weaknesses. Allied to this, they always seem to have positive mindsets towards life generally, but specifically in relation to how they view the leadership role which in turn influences how they act and behave every day. We will look at this aspect more closely in Chapter 6.

- **Who they are.** Genuine Leaders have strengths across a number of vital personal characteristics or traits that are vital in any leadership context. They always seem to have attributes that draw others to them, and which help them to a build a meaningful partnership with their people in order to achieve the planned results. This will be our focus in Chapter 7.
- **What they do.** Genuine Leaders are of course multi-skilled, but they will always tell you that they view these skills as being the icing on the cake, not much good if the cake is not there. We will consider some of these skills in Chapter 8.

All this talk about the right stuff raises an age-old question which is worth a quick digression. Can everyone become a Genuine Leader? Ah yes, it is that old chestnut again, the nature–nurture dilemma. Are top leaders born or made? Certainly, leadership skills can be learned and developed, so in that sense, Genuine Leaders can be made. But is it possible to change personal qualities, or an individual's mindset? To some degree it probably is, but never easily and not in the short term. Mindsets and attributes cannot be learned or changed in the same way that skills can because these aspects of our make-up are the product of a lifetime's development and perhaps, in some part, even inherited it is often argued.

So, there must be some natural foundation there because when an individual lacks the right outlook or certain personal qualities, hoping to be a great leader is an unattainable goal and no amount of leadership training

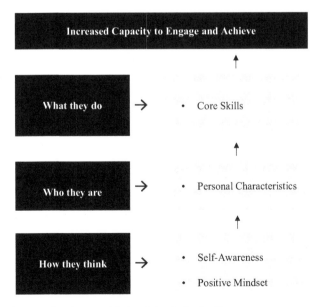

Figure 2.2 Genuine Leaders are Made of the Right Stuff

will compensate for their absence. In that sense there is a born component, so you might say that Genuine Leaders are born and made.

As we will see, the more of the right stuff that an individual has, the more likely they can make it to the level of Genuine Leadership. The less of it, the greater the likelihood they will end up operating in Impostor mode most of the time.

Summary

Leaders come in all shapes and sizes, but their success is measured against some common expectations. Can they engage their people to the maximum possible and then translate that into higher productivity to achieve the best results? And can they do it in a sustained manner. Clearly, every leader's performance is prone to fluctuations – they are not robots – but overall patterns of effectiveness help to define what I believe are two positive groupings of leaders and two categories of Impostors.

Genuine Leaders outshine others in large part because they have more of the right stuff to lead which helps them to balance the engage-achieve relationship most of the time. Nearly Leaders have some work to do if they are to maximize their potential. The Impostors – Deflating and Toxic – are who they are because, to varying degrees, they lack the right stuff which causes them to underperform, be that in relation to engaging people, or in the level of results they deliver or occasionally both.

The following chapters will take an in-depth look at each of the eight leader-types found in the Leadership Wheel and will describe the most frequently seen attitudes and behaviors relevant to each type. Of course, in real life, not every leader will share all the strengths or suffer from all the weaknesses associated with a given category, but they will have a fair smattering of them. In later chapters, we will also return to explore the elements of the right stuff in greater detail.

Notes

1 Fiona Macrae, 'I'm the Chimpion! Ape Trounces the Best of the Human World in Memory Competition.' *Daily Mail*, online edition. January 26, 2008. www.dailymail.co.uk/news/article-510260/Im-chimpion–Ape-trounces-best-human-world-memory-competition.html. Accessed August 18, 2020.
2 Jeffrey K. Rohrs, 'Pandora's Box of Loyalty.' September 10, 2012. www.mediapost.com/publications/article/182614/pandoras-box-of-loyalty.html. Accessed August 18, 2020.
3 BrainyQuote. www.brainyquote.com/quotes/anita_roddick_385165. Accessed August 18, 2020.
4 Tom Wolfe, *The Right Stuff* (New York: Farrar, Straus, and Giroux, 1979).

Chapter 3

The True Face of Leadership

Over the years, I have been fortunate to meet and learn from many Genuine Leaders at all enterprise levels. To build a better picture of the failings seen in Impostors, it would be helpful to begin by more clearly understanding the positive face of leadership. In other words, before exploring its dark side, we need to see leadership's true face. We will turn our attention in this chapter to the positive leader categories found in the Leadership Wheel – Genuine and Nearly Leaders. Beginning with an examination of the Genuine Leaders, for they are the ultimate role models, the content highlights what it is that helps them to outpace others. The focus then shifts to the Nearly Leaders to discover what they do well, but also where they slip up.

Genuine Leaders Are the Elite

Once upon a time it was a badge of honor to be considered part of an 'elite.' This is not true today. In these politically charged times, thinking in terms of elites is a lot less acceptable. The term is more frequently confused with being elitist which is not such a good thing as it usually means that someone is out of touch or part of some sort of golden circle. Yet, there is nothing wrong with a bit of elitism when it relates to excellence in performance and the recognition of top performers should not just be confined to the sporting world.

Each one of us may well be considered equal under God and the law, but every field of human endeavor has its high achievers, those select few who rise far above the mediocrity seen in the many. No doubt you remember that it was Usain Bolt who won the 100 meters at the last Olympics, but do you remember who posted the slowest time in the heats? I did not think so. In leadership terms too, all are most definitely not equal and Genuine Leaders are the chosen few. They excel in the role, are a step above other leaders, and are the very best that an organization has to offer, serving as examples for others in terms of their mindset, attributes, and skills. They deserve recognition for that fact and in my opinion too little acknowledgement is given to these, often unsung, leaders within organizations. Perhaps if more fuss was made of their achievements there would be greater pressure on underperforming leaders to get their act together.

Underpinning their success, in the first instance, is the fact that Genuine Leaders think very differently about the leadership role. When you talk to them about leading others, they seem to instinctively get the point that employees may well work for organizations, but they are inspired towards greater achievement by other people. These leaders accept that if employees are to be enticed towards achieving organizational goals then they must first be attracted to them, as individuals, by the way they think, which in turn affects how they act and behave. They very much operate from the leader-partner frame of mind, as opposed to the leader–follower mindset.

Genuine Leaders have the ability to consistently make things happen in practice, in terms of the engage–achieve link, because when you spend time in their company you see that not only do they have plenty of the right stuff, but that they use it to *influence* and not to *dominate* others. They come across as passionate individuals who 'connect' easily with colleagues and employees, getting them to buy into what they are trying to achieve. They are often – although not exclusively – charismatic, and when they are, I have found that there is plenty of substance to back up the style. In all cases, they are self-confident, without the cockiness that often attaches itself to that quality. Always calm and controlled, these leaders never rely on aggression to get what they want. At the same time employees intuitively recognize that they are no pushovers either. They know where the line is and rarely cross it.

While employees might initially be drawn to Genuine Leaders because of the force of their personality, what seems to sustain that commitment is the fact that these leaders can deliver results. Critically, they can translate the positive relationships they develop with their employees into higher productivity and have the capacity to manage day to day operations in an efficient and effective manner. As a result, they deliver on the expectations of both superiors and subordinates.

Naturally, not all Genuine Leaders are the same and there is no common mold or template to describe one, they are individual characters with different personalities. What I believe is common to them all, however, is their talent for engaging and achieving and in doing so they successfully balance our three dimensions of work. What differentiates them is simply how good they are at getting that balance right. As in any walk of life, there are always some who are better than others.

Broadly, the two types of Genuine Leaders that I have commonly seen in organizations are shown in Figure 3.1.

Nurturers

Most of the Genuine Leaders can be described as Nurturers. On first hearing this description, you would be forgiven for thinking that I am promoting these leaders are some sort of 'mother hens,' but that is not the case at all. Yes, Nurturers are balanced and team-oriented individuals who show real

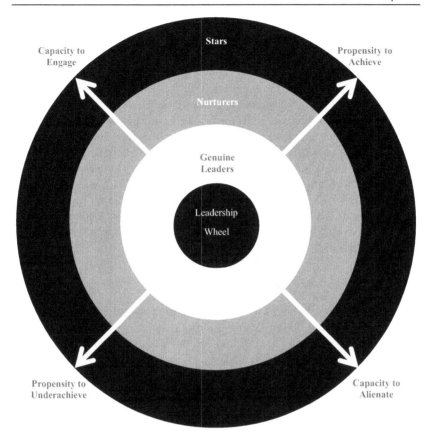

Figure 3.1 Two Types of Genuine Leaders

concern for the well-being of their employees. They truly value their people. But when you interact with them, you also quickly notice that they are very determined to achieve high quality results and are never prepared to accept second best or shoddy performance. So, they do like to help their people grow and develop, but they also expect a lot in return.

Although not necessarily the most charismatic of leaders, Nurturers engage others through their strength of character, warm personalities, and the positive relationships they build with them. They are hard-working and dedicated, bringing a positive energy and enthusiasm to everything they do. These leaders strive to adopt what I would call an engaging style of leadership most of the time, as their self-confidence enables them to create an inclusive environment where employees are involved in decision making and have opportunities to use their initiative in their roles. Nurturers are not afraid to empower their people and provide them with appropriate levels of autonomy depending upon the circumstances involved. They also possess high levels of integrity and never have hidden agendas, which helps them to generate strong loyalty from their employees, because they always know where they stand. Employees respond well to Nurturers simply because, in words that I have heard expressed many times, they feel valued as human beings.

Yet, for all of this, Nurturers expect their people to deliver on expectations. They do not tolerate underperformance, are prepared to confront it head on, but when doing so they seem capable of getting their point across without having to resort to aggressive behaviors. Employees quickly recognize when they have stepped over the line and are given ample opportunities to improve, with appropriate support when required. However, Nurturers will not be taken for fools either, and those who consistently fail to deliver on expectations will not be endured for long because these leaders recognize that to do so will only affect the productivity and motivation of others. In that sense, they are most definitely not mother hens.

Stars

Stars are always in the minority within organizations for they are the truly exceptional leaders. You do not come across them very often, but when you do, they stand out a mile. In fact, they are the minority of the minority that I mentioned earlier. These leaders have the same desire to engage with their teams as Nurturers do, but in my experience, what sets them apart is that they also possess a strongly inspirational quality about them. They are those special few individuals who have a natural gift of being able to really lift employees. Their positive attitude to life and boundless energy are infectious and they attract like-minded individuals to them. Stars are usually very charismatic leaders, yet they seem to lack any trace of arrogance. A few of the Stars that I have met were not overly charismatic, but they still had incredible ability to inspire others through the power of their intellect or the scale of their ideas. In all cases, these leaders gain the complete commitment of their employees based again on a partnership-based approach.

Stars tend to be 'big picture' characters that can see where the team needs to go, yet they can translate this general vision into meaningful and compelling common goals. Although they may not always be as strong as Nurturers at dealing with the more mundane aspects of work, they ensure that things get done. If not comfortable themselves with this area, then they make sure that those strengths are available within the team to compensate. I would describe the leadership style favored by Stars for most of the time as *facilitating*, for they allow their teams high levels of autonomy and freedom of action. This, of course, takes time to build up because employees need to be ready for this approach, but the philosophy of Stars is clearly to empower their employees to the highest level possible. As a result, they can bring the best out of their people.

At the same time, Stars do not tolerate underperformance of any kind either. Like the Nurturers, they are prepared to deal with individual or collective shortcomings and can do so in a controlled manner. Aggression again does not feature in their approach, but they do not need it. Often their employees strive to give their best because they just do not want to let them down, not through fear of retribution, but of out of a sense of loyalty.

Working for both types of Genuine Leaders is a deeply enriching experience most of the time because they create a work environment which is based on collective ownership and mutual achievement. Certainly, the morale, motivation, and levels of engagement that I have seen among employees working for these leaders is always impressive. For Nurturers and Stars, it is their overall ability to combine the leadership and management functions which defines them. It is largely their levels of charisma and ability to inspire which differentiate them from one another. People feel valued when working for both these leaders, yet at the same time recognize that they are expected to perform. Genuine Leaders certainly do not run holiday camps. Employees are required, yet also seem very willing, to give more because they feel part of something bigger than themselves and they know from experience that their extra effort does not go unnoticed. That said, these leaders remain human and have their off days, but the general pattern of their behavior really engages employees and gets great results. Unfortunately, there are far too few Genuine Leaders in organizations today.

The Nearly Leaders

Except for school sports days, there are rarely any prizes given out for almost doing something well. As the saying goes, nearly never won the race, so it may seem somewhat unusual not to treat the Nearly Leaders as Impostors. After all, success as a leader is not about almost doing things well, and like being half-pregnant, it is reasonable to assume that being a nearly successful leader is just not possible.

Although they do not deserve the same acclaim as Genuine Leaders, I believe that these leaders do warrant positive recognition because they are generally doing their best to apply effective leadership approaches. They should, at the very least, be credited for that. Like the Genuine Leaders, they believe in engaging their employees and tend to succeed in that regard, albeit this can be short-lived sometimes. Unfortunately, due to several important failings, these leaders tend to underachieve in terms of the results they deliver for the organization.

Yet, in spite of the fact that they lack the talents or levels of consistency seen in the best leaders, it would be unfair to treat them as Impostors because on the whole they do make a positive contribution and, more importantly, with the right guidance and support they have the potential to develop into Genuine Leaders.

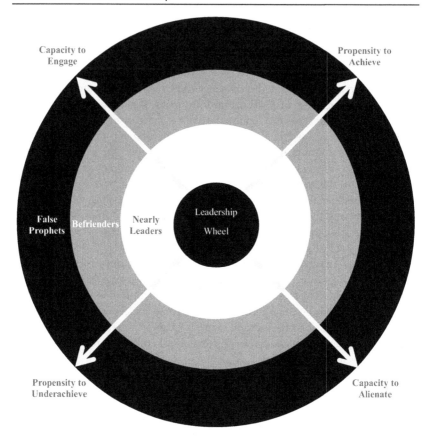

Figure 3.2 Two Types of Nearly Leaders

Nearly Leaders are *good for people* because they strive to fully engage with their employees. They are *not as good for process and performance* in the sense that they cannot always get things done to the level possible. They do not consistently convert their positive relationships with employees into the highest productivity achievable. So, they do add value for the organization, but they could deliver more. The general types of Nearly Leaders that I have seen are shown in Figure 3.2.

Befrienders

Befrienders are like Nurturers in that they aim to forge good relationships with employees, based on having a pleasant and engaging personality. However, they differ in one critical way in my experience. These leaders are somewhat too passive. They lack the degree of self-confidence seen in

Nurturers and as a result they build relationships with their people, not necessarily because they see it as the best approach, but in some ways they do so as a form of defense mechanism. Befrienders often fall into the trap of believing that if they 'get on well' with their employees then they will respond to this and that the work will be done to the standard required. While this might seem like an approach that should work, it does not in most cases because they over-rely on the bonds they have with their employees as their source of power and authority.

I have noticed how Befrienders frequently have an exaggerated fear of being unpopular that results in them striving for harmony with their people and they do their utmost to maintain it, sometimes at all costs. For example, when you talk with them about work-related matters, these leaders are overly concerned with how their employees will respond to something they are planning to do, or they get unnecessarily stressed if their teams seem down or de-motivated on occasion which in reality is going to happen from time to time no matter how good the leader is.

This desire to sustain positive relations frequently causes Befrienders to ignore underperformance or to fail to act when things are not going the way they want. Usually they compensate for this by doing extra work themselves, or more likely by an over-dependence on a few members of their team with whom they have a particularly close relationship. As a rule, these leaders have a propensity to sidestep challenging issues rather than confront them head on and difficult decisions or situations where potential for conflict is high are avoided, or at best long fingered. This softly, softly approach adopted by Befrienders also creates an environment where consensus is sought on every major issue, which is not only time consuming, but can also lead to a situation which I would describe as the 'tail wagging the dog.'

This leadership approach causes problems in the long run as their employees sense that it is they who are ultimately in control. Particularly, I have seen how the more dominant characters in the team can take advantage of this which in turn raises questions among remaining employees as to who is really in charge. Here is an example of the kind of difficulties that one Befriender whom I coached in the past allowed himself to run into:

A new head accountant was appointed as the leader of the finance department in a medium-sized engineering firm. The position involved assuming responsibility for a small team of accountants, a business analyst, a purchasing supervisor, and a couple of administration assistants. The previous head had been in the position for a long time but had recently retired. The new head accountant had been with the company for a few years and was the de-facto assistant to the previous head, but never held any official title. As such this was his first senior leadership appointment.

After taking on the new role, the new head accountant felt there was not any real need to make changes as the team seemed to be working well, so he mainly just offered support and guidance when required. He worked hard to build positive relationships with his people, often turning a blind eye to some things he was unhappy about because he did not want to, in his own words, 'rock the boat' too soon.

Most of the team responded well to this and relationships for the most part were initially good. However, after several months, the new head accountant began to have frequent confrontations with one of the senior accountants, who began to constantly question his decisions, often in front of other members of the team. In order not to let things get out of hand, the head often gave too much leeway to this accountant on the occasions when he challenged him. He frequently changed decisions to placate this guy or allowed him to dominate team meetings.

At first, the new head accountant felt that it was just this one individual who was the problem, but over time he noticed that others in the team also began to adopt similar negative approaches.

Increasingly Befrienders can allow their leadership credentials with their team to be eroded, particularly when the stronger members are given too free a rein. All of this naturally diminishes their ability to fully engage their people and the collective impact of these shortcomings means that teams led by Befrienders fail to deliver the level of performance possible. That is why they underachieve. Often their superiors can see them as being 'too nice.'

Befrienders are more commonly seen in early career stages when as new leaders they are finding it hard to come to terms with certain aspects of the role. Like the head accountant, they often fall into the trap of allowing their position to be undermined. With support, these leaders can and do transition to Genuine Leadership if they become more assertive and recognize that being an effective leader is not a popularity contest and that at times they must, in order to get better results in the longer term, act in ways or take decisions that may not always be popular with their direct reports in the short run.

False Prophets

False Prophets are the minority in the Nearly Leader category and they have similar personality traits to Stars in the sense that they too are usually strongly charismatic figures who have high energy levels and a natural enthusiasm for life. They are also extroverts who are energized by being around other people. False Prophets seem to love the idea of a challenge and those that I have met were always good at getting people to buy into change and new ideas. Unfortunately, unlike Stars, these leaders seem unable to sustain those high levels of engagement with their teams because they suffer from the major shortcoming of lacking follow-through. This reduces their ability to get things done. They may be great at raising expectations but are not so good at delivering results consistently over the long term.

False Prophets only seem capable of devoting their full attention to any aspect of work or a given project in short bursts before they lose interest and search for something new and more stimulating. They have an aversion to the humdrum aspects of implementation and directing the workload on an ongoing basis. Essentially, they struggle with the managing bit of the role. What is endearing in some ways about these leaders is that they can mask this shortcoming for some time because they are good at using their charms to delegate the mundane and uninteresting tasks to others. In that sense, they overuse their appealing personalities to maintain control and deliver productivity. They believe that their natural magnetism will see them through in all circumstances.

Unfortunately, over time, employees become a bit disillusioned with all the talk and little action by False Prophets. They get frustrated with the lack of results and begin to view these leaders as somewhat superficial charmers. I find that employees do not necessarily turn against them as such – they are hard people to dislike – but it is more a case of feeling let down by them. This erosion of credibility in the eyes of their employees naturally impacts on the standing of False Prophets which has a related effect on overall performance. For this reason, the teams they lead tend to lose their way and that is why as leaders, they underachieve.

Both types of Nearly Leaders are far from a bad bunch in my experience. They do engage with employees, but unless they address their shortcomings, their ability to act as a driving force tends to diminish over time, as employees realize that they are not dealing with a Genuine Leader. These leaders certainly do get results, but not always to the highest level possible and they struggle to sustain above the line performance over the long term.

Nearly Leaders are positive-minded characters, however, so they do add value in that sense and, particularly the Befrienders, can develop their potential to lead and address their shortcomings because they already have a lot of the right stuff. That is why it is unfair to treat them as Impostors. Sometimes, these leaders are better suited to certain support roles such as HR or sales, where their specific talents shine.

Summary

The positive face of leadership is not about being perfect. Nobody can achieve total perfection, but effective leadership is about striving to get as close to that aspiration as possible. Genuine Leaders are closest to the full package; they are notable because they possess all the right stuff to lead and continuously translate that into a real ability to engage and achieve over sustained periods. They know themselves well, looking inward before outward, and they work hard to achieve excellence in their own performance before they expect it of others. But they do expect it of others.

Nearly Leaders are potentially on the right track and with appropriate support, guidance, and a desire to do so, they have the potential to transition to Genuine Leaders. However, without that effort, they run the risk of consistently underperforming and can end up, over the longer term, slipping into Impostor territory.

Armed with a clearer view of what makes a Genuine Leader, the following chapters set about unmasking the Impostors. The challenge in this will not necessarily be in spotting them but in trying to differentiate them. Unraveling their world is hard because they wear different masks, often at the same time. But it is worth the effort to identify their shortcomings, because as Carl Jung said, "Everything that irritates us about others can lead us to an understanding of ourselves."[1]

Note

1 BrainyQuote. www.brainyquote.com/authors/carl-jung-quotes. Accessed August 18, 2020.

Chapter 4

A Darker Side to Leadership

There have been many interesting and indeed bizarre Impostors throughout history. Although somewhat forgotten today, the notorious Count Victor Lustig,[1] who plied his deceptive trade on both sides of the Atlantic in the early 1900s, is one of my all-time favorites. As a conman, he was exceptional and while he may have started on a small scale, he eventually worked his way up to one of the most famous scams of all time.

One of Lustig's early frauds used what he called the money-printing box. To unsuspecting wealthy (and, more accurately, greedy) targets he would show them how the box 'printed' a $100 bill, but while doing so, complained that it took more than six hours to print each one. If only he could get it to work faster, he would lament. The victim, believing that with a bit of patience there was huge money to be made, would purchase the box, usually for a large sum, only to realize twelve hours later that, after the box had produced two more $100 bills, only blank paper came out. By that time, Lustig was long gone of course.

He later graduated to his most celebrated feat, that of selling the Eiffel Tower to an unsuspecting scrap metal dealer while posing as a French government official. A truly remarkable achievement, it must be said. In fact, he came within a whisker of selling it on a second occasion too. At a later stage, Lustig is also said to have convinced Al Capone, the famous gangster, to invest $50,000 in a stock deal. Lustig held the mafia man's money in a bank for two months, then returned it to him, claiming that the deal had fallen through. Impressed with Lustig's honesty, Capone gave him a reward of $5,000, which was the whole idea of the scam in the first place. This guy was a real chancer if ever there was one.

From a less distant era, Frank William Abagnale, Jr.,[2] the notorious con artist upon whom the movie *Catch Me if You Can*[3] is based, also rates highly for his ingenuity and sheer brass neck. His exploits are legendary and include impersonating a doctor and an airline pilot, where he succeeded in flying around the world for free. Now that was some achievement. Frank was eventually caught and has since turned over a new leaf having established a respected consulting company advising corporations on fraud prevention. Poacher turned gamekeeper you might even say.

Just like any fraudster or scam artist, the Impostor Leaders too are pretending to be something they are not and when you talk to them, many believe that they are good leaders. But they are only kidding themselves. Sure, they might be masquerading as Genuine Leaders but for most of the time they are something else entirely. Like many people, you can probably think of a leader where you work – hopefully not yourself – who richly deserves the Impostor tag. You might not be able to quite put your finger on exactly why this is so, but you get the sense with some leaders that they are essentially trying to sell you the Eiffel Tower. Something about them just screams 'fraud.'

At the risk of sounding like a broken record, it is important to emphasize again that all leaders have the capacity to slip into Impostor mode on occasion. But only on occasion and even when they do fail, sometimes it is not really their fault. Underperforming and disengaged employees or stressful situations can bring out Impostor-type behaviors in any leader, pushing them over the edge and driving them to act and behave in ways they would not normally do. That does not make them Impostors, however, because these are just infrequent lapses. All these incidents demonstrate is that they are human. It is only those leaders who continually underperform in a sustained way and get it wrong more times than right when it comes to the engage–achieve relationship that truly deserve the Impostor Leader title.

This chapter focuses on the Deflating Impostors and explores what it is they do that makes them deserve this badge of dishonor. It shows how they underperform when it comes to engaging and achieving largely because of personal failings which mean they lack the capacity to bring the best out in others. Although not necessarily malevolent characters most of the time, the Deflating Impostors do have a cost to organizations in that they fail to achieve the best results possible.

The Deflating Impostors

Deflating Impostors add less value to organizations than they could because they cannot engage effectively with others and are generally underachievers in terms of the results they generate. The causes of their underperformance are many and varied, but largely stem from their own personal shortcomings, which may include, aloofness, insecurity, self-consciousness, or even downright laziness.

In general, I find that these Impostors lack any real ability to inspire others which is compounded by extremely cautious or in some cases negative mindsets. Everything they do is tinged in grey, you could say, and they are at best mediocre performers and at worst soul destroying for those who work for them. Two types of Deflating Impostors are regularly seen (Figure 4.1).

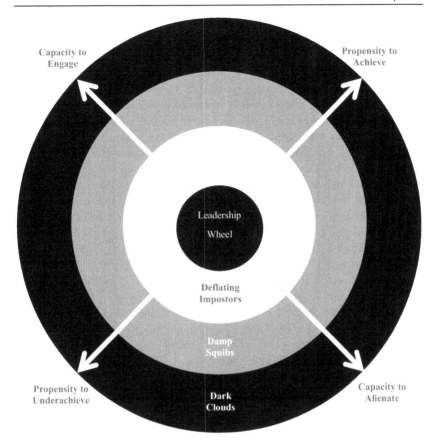

Figure 4.1 Two Types of Deflating Impostors

Damp Squibs

Squibs are small detonating devices that resemble miniature sticks of dynamite. In the past, they had many applications in mining and military fields, and today are more frequently used for creating special effects for movies. Given that they contain a powder-based explosive, keeping them dry is critical; hence a damp squib is one which fails to explode because it is wet.

Damp Squib Impostors constantly fail to ignite. It could be said that they have a tendency to implode. They form most of the Deflating Impostor category and have neither the capacity to fully engage their people, nor to achieve anything but an acceptable level of results. I have come across a fair few of these leaders in my time and they are often slightly introverted individuals who find it impossible to really connect with others. They fail to truly understand where other people are coming from. Although they are not necessarily negative-minded characters, and can often be reasonably upbeat, when you watch their attempts to interrelate with others, it always feels a bit awkward and forced. For sure, Damp Squibs can be quite intelligent, but they usually lack common sense and indeed the human touch. Strangely enough, they frequently delude themselves that they are an inspirational force, even though they are usually the complete opposite.

Damp Squibs are fundamentally insecure characters who lack the required self-assurance to fully empower their employees. Instead of creating a working environment founded upon autonomy and empowerment, they tend to over rely on high levels of direction and control. There is nothing wrong with direction and control of course, and any leader must drive performance on occasions, but in the case of Damp Squibs the reins are never released. From my experience in dealing with them, these Impostors have a propensity to micro-manage their people to such an extent that they eventually become frustrated with the lack of freedom. They are the type of leaders who will 'delegate' a task to an employee but will then essentially stand over their shoulder while they do it, driving them around the twist with their finicky behavior.

As well as their predisposition to control everything due to their insecurities, Damp Squibs do not really deal with people or situations in an open and transparent fashion either. They will often say one thing but think something quite different entirely. When you watch them interact with their people, their sentences are full of the word 'but,' as in "I am not being critical … *but*," which is then followed by a whole series of petty gripes. When faced with difficult situations or indeed people, these leaders will frequently shy away from tackling them directly, instead, they will often try to manipulate events from behind the scenes. In this sense, a lot of them are passive-aggressives who like to operate in the shadows.

For Damp Squibs, decision making is far from their strong point either and for important decisions they can spend as much time weighing up the consequences of potential solutions as they do implementing them. Nothing substantial is done by these Impostors without protracted analysis and little is left to chance. All bases must be covered. Caution is therefore the key word, which has the impact of creating what I would describe as reactive rather than proactive environments. Their inability to take important decisions in a timely fashion also slows down the rate of progress and serves as a further frustration for their people as they wait for an answer.

What is perhaps most annoying about these leaders, judging by the regular stream of feedback I have received over the years from employees stuck working for them, is that some Damp Squibs seem unwilling to show any signs of personal weakness or frailty. This frequently manifests itself, for example, in how they interact with others, particularly their subordinates, on subjects they know little or nothing about. Rather than admit that they are unsure on a given topic, or that someone else might know more than they do about it, Damp Squibs will frequently act as if they are an authority on every issue, making a little bit of knowledge go a long way and throwing in lots of terminology or jargon for good effect. Over time, people see through this of course, but it is hard for someone more junior to confront or to expose them for what they are. But, in the end, this inability to essentially be honest with their people, and indeed human, further erodes their credibility.

Damp Squibs are however able to sustain productivity at a level that keeps them in a job, but there is always untapped potential among the employees who work for them. Most of this slack is picked up by themselves so these leaders put in long hours and are often to be found working late into the evening – which of itself is not a bad thing – were it not for the fact that they would not have to do so if they had not created an unproductive environment in the first place. This does get them kudos from their superiors though when in reality it is more likely a sign of their inability to trust others enough to delegate properly to them. In addition, Damp Squibs are usually finely tuned into the world of organizational politics, not necessarily out of any great sense of loyalty, but rather as a tool for self-advancement. They are fence-sitters who have a knack for picking the right side of an argument, subtly changing sides at opportune moments. For certain, they are rarely to be found taking an isolated position. Sometimes their ability to 'play the game' can help them progress in organizations which are strongly political.

Here is an example of one Damp Squib in action which I believe highlights very well the overall mindset of these leaders:

> I recently encountered the following incident in a large private sector organization. A new leader had taken over an existing team and instead of getting everyone together to provide them with an overview of where he was coming from, he sent each employee a list of 'team rules' by email which he expected them to abide by. This memo, several pages long, covered everything from attendance at meetings, how to raise an issue with him, to believe it or not, rules on how to structure and write an email. The rules section ended with a subtle threat that he would be monitoring individual performance against these expectations in the coming months.
>
> Yet, bizarrely, at the same time, the closing paragraph of the email read like an excerpt from the script for the movie *Braveheart*, with a call to arms about how with him on board they were going to climb mountains together.

Undoubtedly, there must be some guidance given as to what employees can and cannot do, but the means of communication is usually as important as the message itself. Writing an email, and such a long one at that, to an existing team, many of whom had been in the organization for several years was classic Damp Squib behavior. Apart from the fact that the 'rules' were completely lost on the employees, the approach simply served to annoy and frustrate them. The William Wallace impression at the end was met with outright mockery. As an introduction to their new boss, it was certainly far from ideal, yet it typifies the kind of thing that Damp Squibs will do. In this particular case, when discussing the issue with him, the leader in question could not see anything wrong with his approach and genuinely thought it the best way to reach everyone without having to "drag them away from their desks for too long." Indeed.

This might seem like a trifling incident, and on its own it probably was. It mattered because it was but a snapshot of the overall and repetitive pattern of behavior adopted by this Impostor. It also provides a very good example of the kind of thing that all Damp Squibs will do. This particular guy represents a fine specimen of these leaders. Personally, he was very ambitious which is often the case with Damp Squibs but, like most of them, he could not communicate his vision effectively, or get others to buy into what he wanted to achieve.

Over time, constant exposure to the kind of pedantic and distant behavior typified by this incident only served to disengage many of his employees. Yet, he somehow remained oblivious to the impact he was having on them. When he did bring them together, rather than strive for meaningful two-way communication, he often launched into endless monologues while his team fidgeted or stared despairingly at the floor. But he could come out of such meetings and make comments like "I think that went well," while his employees were literally banging their heads off the wall in another room. For me, Damp Squibs seem to live in a parallel universe at times.

The cumulative effect of their bland, controlling nature and general tendency to have their finger in every pie is that certain employees find Damp Squibs simply impossible to work under for very long. Ambitious individuals with lots of enthusiasm and initiative quickly grow tired of the reactive, nit-picking approach adopted by them. They feel smothered by the lack of empowerment or autonomy which defines life under these Impostors and having to constantly deal with a leader who craves approval but does not know how to earn it. This is, I believe, one of the great dangers with Damp Squibs in that they demoralize high-potential managers and employees for whom they are responsible. Although they can spot potential just as well as the next person, these Impostors frequently do their very best to nullify not nurture it, as they are afraid of being overshadowed. They constantly throw up meaningless obstacles in order to rein talented individuals in.

On the other hand, for needy individuals who like lots of hand holding, Damp Squibs can seem quite appealing. Certain people do like to work in heavily structured or controlled environments. Unfortunately, this type of individual tends to be an average performer. The consequence of this, over the long term, is that as the more talented characters jump ship, they are often replaced by these mediocre recruits who can cope with working under a Damp Squib. This in turn means that teams led by these Impostors tend to underachieve because the work environment becomes very rule bound, reactive, and lacking in creativity.

Dark Clouds

Dark Clouds possess many of the same personal failings as Damp Squibs, and they too suffer from a general inability to engage employees or to achieve high performance. What particularly differentiates these leaders, though, is that they are extremely negative-minded characters that do as little as they can get away with. You might think that anyone with all these deficiencies would be quickly found out, and in commercial enterprises they tend not to survive for too long today. However, they thrive in places like the public sector, where I have seen a fair few Dark Clouds hanging around. They rarely progress beyond low to mid-levels on the ladder, and usually, they reach those positions because they were next in line, as opposed to having the right skills or aptitude for the role.

These Impostors are predominantly unfulfilled individuals who seem dissatisfied with where their life is going, or indeed has ended up. They secretly harbor dreams of doing something completely different, or for the lazy ones, nothing at all. Their lack of drive and obsessive fear of risk prevents them acting on their desires, although if you listen to them the fault for their personal circumstances usually lies elsewhere. As a result, they are often glum, moody, and inconsistent performers who are frequently the cynics in the organization with a tendency to wallow in self-pity. Dark Clouds are tremendously uninspiring characters who take no ownership for their own failings and they project a general air of despondency about them. They are the type of people who can suck the energy out of a room just by their presence.

Part of the problem for Dark Clouds, or certainly those that I have interacted with, is that they have terrible relationship management skills. They cannot relate to people at anything other than a superficial level. They are not leaders in any true sense of the word, and in fact they are often shirkers who abdicate the leadership role, their employees certainly seem to feel a strong sense of alienation from them. These Impostors also avoid taking decisions, or when they do, they are simply hopeless at follow through. Rather than delegating to their employees, they are best described as offloaders. Here is an example of one Dark Cloud that I came across:

> In one public sector organization that I worked with the boss of a section was as Dark a Cloud as you can ever imagine. She was a very despondent character, known for her negativity and moodiness among her employees. Some days were okay, whereas others could be difficult depending upon her mood. On the good days, she would arrive with a degree of normality,

whereas on others she brought a complete air of misery into the office. Unfortunately, the bad days far outweighed the good.

Each day as she arrived for work in the car park, her employees would look out of the office window to determine what sort of humor they thought she was in. The result of this observation would set the tone for the day within the office!

Although an extreme case, this Dark Cloud created an environment of utter dejection in the office. She was not necessarily aggressive with others, but due to her moodiness, she could be very abrupt on occasions and completely distant from her team. Of course, she might have been clinically depressed, and she certainly had low energy levels, but that is not the point. Apart from her own poor productivity she instilled a sense of underperformance in all those who worked for her.

Working for Dark Clouds is somewhat akin to being hit with a wet fish daily and the work environment they create is best described as mind-numbing. Positive and motivated individuals cannot stand working for them, with the result that, over time, these Impostors will build teams which are equivalent to the living dead, full of low performers doing just enough to get by. Employees that work for these Impostors are usually individuals who also lack any real motivation or enthusiasm for their job. They figure out what the required level of performance is and stick with that for they know nothing above the norm will be expected most of the time. Essentially, they can plod through the working day.

Both types of Deflating Impostors can significantly reduce organizational performance, or at the very least, there is always a lot of scope for increased productivity among the people working for them. The Damp Squibs can deliver an acceptable level of results, but they only discover the tip of the iceberg in comparison to what better leaders could achieve with the same resources. Dark Clouds can take the joy out of working life. They rarely survive for long in commercial life today, but they can be found elsewhere.

Summary

There can be a bit of the Deflating Impostor in all leaders, but as said before, it only surfaces occasionally in the better ones. Damp Squibs and Dark Clouds are who they are most of the time. Although, the Damp Squibs might infrequently display some genuine leadership behaviors, they never do so in any sustained way and when they do something well, my goodness do they never stop talking about it.

In their defense, Deflating Impostors do not always consciously cause damage in organizations but cause it they do all the same. Most of those that I have encountered were not overtly nasty characters either; they demoralized and disheartened employees as opposed to targeting individuals for abuse on a daily basis. But I have witnessed how they are not always completely pain-free in that regard either and can resort to underhanded tactics particularly when feeling threatened, or if they come under pressure. They might lack the guts to confront issues in an open manner, but they can compensate for that through a mean streak.

Like any individual, there is potential for the Deflating Impostors to change and improve, but they find it very difficult to do so because many of the causes of their underperformance are deeply rooted in their personalities. They are not unskilled or untalented individuals, or at least the Damp Squibs are not, but they lack aspects of the right stuff such as a positive mindset or those attributes which can serve as a magnetic force for others. These are not so easily changed and developed.

The following chapter focuses on the Toxic Impostors and explores the damage that they cause both to individuals and the organizations they work for, and shows how these leaders are more malicious by nature in how they go about their job.

Notes

1 'Victor Lustig.' Wikipedia. Last modified August, 14, 2020. https://en.wikipedia.org/wiki/Victor_Lustig. Accessed August 18, 2020.
2 'Frank Abagnale.' Wikipedia. Last modified July 29, 2020. https://en.wikipedia.org/wiki/Frank_Abagnale. Accessed August 18, 2020.
3 *Catch Me if You Can*, directed and produced by Steven Spielberg (DreamWorks Pictures, 2002). See www.netflix.com/ch-en/title/60024942.

Chapter 5

When Leaders Go Bad

Until she died, 'Trouble' lived a happy life, or at least a reasonably contented one you would have to say.[1] The much-loved white Maltese terrier belonging to Leona Helmsley, the billionaire hotelier,[2] was bequeathed $12 million in her will, more money, in fact, than Mrs Helmsley initially left to her brother or indeed to any of her relatives for that matter. Then, poor old Trouble had to face a fair bit of trouble of her own.

She started receiving anonymous death threats, or more accurately her keeper got them on her behalf. Apparently about 20 to 30 in all were received, ranging from 'I'm gonna kill the dog' to 'I'm gonna kidnap the dog. I need the $12 million.' Things got worse still for the little terrier, as she later lost $10 million of the loot in a court settlement. Still, it is fair to assume that there were ample funds left to provide for a happy canine retirement until the pooch's demise. Trouble's life story certainly does give entirely new meaning to 'living a dog's life,' that is for sure.

Being Mrs Helmsley's dog clearly had significant rewards. Being her employee did not. Certainly, Trouble seemed to get the better deal from Leona, if her nickname of 'the Queen of Mean' is anything to go by. She earned this ignominious title in part due to the way she treated her people and for the fact that she was once quoted as saying that 'only the little people pay taxes.' Stories of her alleged abusive treatment of employees are legendary. In one particularly nasty incident it was claimed that, during breakfast at one of her hotels, a waiter brought a cup of tea to the table but had spilled some of the contents onto the saucer. Apparently, her highness grabbed the cup from the poor unfortunate and smashed it on the floor, then demanded that he kneel down and beg for his job. Not the kind of boss you would like to work for, by all accounts.

Leadership does indeed have a darkest side, the family secret, the taboo subject that everyone avoids discussing, if possible. Hidden away in an upstairs room are to be found the Toxic Impostors. This chapter exposes those leaders who, although they achieve results, make life difficult or worse for those unfortunate enough to work for them. Because on the face of it they make the numbers stack up, they are often tolerated or even lauded in certain organizations, but there are always significant costs associated with them.

The Toxic Impostors

Toxic Impostors have either low capabilities in sustaining relationships with employees, or a low desire to do so. The behaviors seen in these leaders are naturally varied, but it can be said that they reflect the worst of those seen in the school playground, except that they carry these juvenile behaviors into adult life. In them can be found a range of destructive conduct including petty jealousy, sycophantism, bravado, bullying, and downright childishness to name but a few.

Through their attitudes and behaviors, I have seen how Toxic Impostors damage their employees, and this can range from low-level but continuous intimidation to a high level, where it manifests itself as bullying. These Impostors reduce the motivation, well-being, job satisfaction, and ultimately the engagement levels of employees. They cannot inspire and make little effort to do so, but they do drive performance usually by creating a culture of fear and distrust. In doing so they send out a message that this is a place where only the toughest survive.

Toxic Impostors may pay lip service to how they value their people because they are smart enough to know that this is what they should be doing. But they do not believe a word of it and based on my dealings with them they actually do the opposite a lot of the time, displaying complete and utter ignorance as to what is required to get the best from people today. Okay, so they do not beat or whip their employees (some would, if they could get away with it) but what they do can be worse in emotional terms for those unfortunate enough to have to deal with them every day. Toxic Impostors see employees not as partners in achieving goals but as vehicles to facilitate their achievement. Results are essentially achieved on the backs of others.

A common thread between all Toxic Impostors is that they are always aggressive characters – overtly or covertly – who seek to dominate those around them (as we shall see, what differentiates the two types of Toxic Impostors is essentially how they apply their aggression).

Toxic Impostors, in my experience, are all about dominance. They believe that if they project themselves as the strongest or brightest person around, then few will challenge them. For them, it is all about winning and losing. They are sore losers.

Two types of Toxic Impostors are frequently found in organizations (Figure 5.1).

Egotists

Salvador Dalí once proclaimed: "Each morning I wake and I experience again a supreme pleasure, the pleasure of being Salvador Dalí."[3] He certainly did not suffer from insecurity, but at least his talent as an artist was in direct proportion to his ego. Egotists are the Salvador Dalís of organizational life,

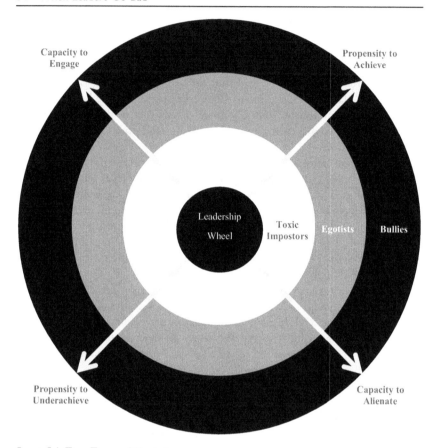

Figure 5.1 Two Types of Toxic Impostors

sharing as they do his aura of grandiosity and believing themselves to be enormously talented individuals. Unlike the great artist, there is usually a gaping hole between their sense of self-worth and reality. Sometimes, they also fool their superiors on this and are fast-tracked within the organization, never hanging around long enough in any one position to be fully measured. Despite their outward displays of cockiness, I have found many Egotists to be quite insecure individuals, although they would certainly never admit to it.

Egotists believe themselves to be charismatic people but that is because they have usually mistaken charisma for arrogance. They use their mis-guided self-image and forceful personalities as weapons to control those around them. Totally self-centered characters, they may well be intelligent but are never as bright as they like to think they are. In general terms, Egotists are calculating and manipulative by nature and are constantly on the lookout for how they can advance their own agenda, usually at the expense of others. They can, when it is in their interest to do so, exude plenty of charm which many people fall for but there is always a sickly-sweet quality about them that leaves a bit of an aftertaste. When charm does not work though, they will quickly revert to type and find another more underhanded way to get what they want.

Egotists are also strongly opinionated individuals who will speak frequently and forcefully regardless of whether they have something of value to contribute. In fact, that is often a secondary concern to them as being heard is generally more important than being right. I have had the misfortune on more than one occasion to sit through the gospel according to an Egotist. There is rarely any other opinion in the room of equivalent status as theirs, except that is, when the boss is around when they can turn into downright sycophants.

If allowed, and often they are because they hoodwink people with their outward signs of leadership, I have watched with interest how Egotists strive to surround themselves with 'fans' – individuals who are neither a threat to them nor question their actions – so they often end up creating an inner circle of 'yes people.' This not only seems to help massage their ego, but it allows them to drive performance as their decisions or actions largely go unchallenged. It also helps them to deliver results which is what makes them seem like good leaders. Being part of this inner circle can be equivalent to membership of a mutual admiration society or participation in some sort of sycophantic love-in; those outside of it feel a strong sense of exclusion and alienation. These fans will however work their backsides off for these Impostors because they somehow fall for all the outward appearances of leadership that Egotists project. They cannot see what really lies behind the façade.

Egotists are not overtly aggressive individuals and they have the ability to maintain a degree of self-control, so they are often very subtle in how they apply their aggression. But they are nasty characters nonetheless. Although they are rarely the type who rant and rave, they are far too calculating for that, they can still be quite cutting and sarcastic with their employees particularly those outside the inner circle. Employees generally live on edge because they know that mistakes are not seen by these leaders as an opportunity for learning, but for one of punishment. Any under-performance is likely to result in disproportionate criticism or ridicule, usually delivered in front of others, because Egotists like audiences when they dish out retribution. Here is an example of an Egotist in action:

> The CEO of a large company I consulted with asked one of his department heads to work on a special project which had significant importance to the organization's future. It involved preparing a feasibility study for a new investment and the CEO wanted it completed in a very short period.

The department head allocated the required tasks to his various direct reports who worked night and day to finalize the project. One individual on the team did constructively question as to whether it was feasible to meet the deadline, but he was sharply informed that the choice was to do the work or leave the team.

The department head himself had little or no input into the preparations, except to come in at a late stage to make significant changes, which put further pressure on his team. However, they pulled out all the stops and had the work done on time – and to a high standard. At the presentation to the CEO and certain board members, the department head and his team outlined their results. The feedback was very positive, and the CEO was glowing in his praise. The department head took all the credit, never once mentioning the input of his team either during the meeting or afterwards.

His only feedback after the event was to launch into severe criticism of that one member of the team who had questioned him previously, because there was a problem with another aspect of his work which arose only because he spent the previous couple of weeks devoting most of his attention to this special initiative.

Taken in isolation, this might again seem like a minor incident, and certainly, had it been a one-off, it would warrant little attention. But this example was symptomatic of an overall, continuous pattern of behavior displayed by this department head, a pure Egotist. He always took all the credit, hogged the limelight at every opportunity, over-relied on his people but never acknowledged their contribution. Feedback, when offered, was usually negative or sarcastic in tone. The word 'thanks' seemed not to exist in his vocabulary.

Not only are Egotists hopeless at giving feedback but they hate to be put under the microscope either, so receiving feedback is anathema to them. They will not accept any form of criticism, or questioning of their decisions, no matter how well intentioned. Instead, they see it as a personal attack. On top of that, they are usually highly territorial people and can quickly become hostile to anyone attempting, as they see it, to undermine them. Once they take a dislike to someone, and it does not take much to get on their wrong side they will lead a concerted, if usually hidden, campaign to get them and they will knowingly sabotage the efforts of others just to pay them back. This is further evidence of their propensity to use covert aggression to get their way and for that reason, they are frequently the organizational back stabbers who are dangerous people to cross.

Working for Egotists is frustrating and demoralizing for most employees because they realize that they are of secondary concern to these leaders. Life under Egotists is akin to walking on eggshells because their people learn that it takes little to earn their wrath. Over time their employees, particularly those outside the inner circle, recognize that they are simply pawns in the bigger game of advancement for the Egotist. They come to understand that these Impostors are shallow, superficial individuals who care only about themselves.

Bullies

Bullies are the worst of the Impostor Leaders. They can be bitter, angry, and even unstable characters who suffer from many of the same failings seen in Egotists. They are largely differentiated from them because they seek to dominate others through their overtly threatening behaviors. Often mildly, if not severely paranoid, Bullies are openly aggressive characters who lack self-control and as a result tend to explode with rage. Generally, they view work life as a constant battle – one which must be won at all costs – and they seem to enjoy inflicting pain on others. Sometimes it appears that they build themselves up by having someone else to knock down. These leaders survive (and in a few cases thrive) in organizations because they drive performance through fear and intimidation.

The arrogant and abrasive nature of Bullies makes them appear confident, but in reality a lot of them, like the Egotists, are insecure individuals who mask that insecurity by trying to show how tough they are. They are often cowards too and when really confronted by someone they can back down but will hold a grudge against that person indefinitely. A lot of people are afraid of Bullies, so they are rarely challenged.

Although Bullies may be a tiny minority in most organizations, there are many respected studies which show that they certainly do exist. And bullies do not necessarily treat all their employees equally badly however but, just like the Egotists, can have favorites who escape the worst of their behavior and others who bear the brunt of it. With them, people are either 'in' or 'out.' If in, then an employee is likely to be spared the worst of their excesses; if out, they become the Bully's target. There are no rules for admission to the 'in club,' and it is exclusively at the behest of the Bully (plus the membership rules frequently change, in line with their generally unstable natures).

Working for Bullies is never a pleasant experience, even when not the target of their abuse. If directly in their sights, individuals can experience severe emotional consequences just like the tormented child in the playground. Even if not in the firing line, Bullies create a stressful environment for everyone, and fear of failure drives performance as opposed to any desire to excel. These Impostors justify their existence by the results they achieve and even if their superiors try to tone down their behavior, they know that as long as the numbers look good they are likely to be retained, once they restrain themselves from doing something completely unacceptable or illegal. Very few organizations get rid of people who deliver on targets, even when it is well known that these leaders come with a lot of unwanted baggage attached.

Employees see this too, and that goes a long way to explaining why it takes so much for an employee to formally complain about Bullies. Here is an example of the kind of thing I am talking about:

> Remember our young leader mentioned in the Preface, whose boss hated him? He certainly worked under a Bully, and in fact he faced the worst kind. Eventually, unable to deal with the ongoing abuse, he did complain to a more senior executive in the organization. The Bully was reprimanded about his behavior, but unsurprisingly kept his job. The direct abuse did reduce after the complaint. However, the young manager was then subtly ostracized by a certain portion of the management team. "Nobody likes snitches" was one of the snide comments made to him by another manager.

Playground stuff or what? Yet, in the end, it was the young manager who left the organization, not the Bully.

Bullies Poison the Atmosphere

Not only do Bullies damage those who report to them, but they can create problems for their peers too. They are rarely collaborative individuals, and to compete with them, other leaders are often forced to fight back, so to speak, with the result that the atmosphere in organizations where Bullies exert high influence can become very tense. I once consulted for a large company in the transport sector where the general manager was a severe Bully. He had been in place for many years and over that time, the dynamic among the management team had changed almost beyond recognition. Many positive leaders, who did not like the poisoned environment being created left the organization and were usually replaced by individuals who more closely matched this Impostor's ideal leadership profile (i.e. other Bullies).

Over a period of a few years, the leadership team at this company transformed from one with a mix of personalities, to one with an overweighting of aggressive and abrasive characters. It was like walking into a lions' den. Oddly enough, most of them loved this environment because Bullies like nothing more than to test their mettle against others. For more junior leaders and employees in the company, it was far from a welcome change however and it was unsurprising that towards the end of this Bully's reign, the organization experienced significant falls in customer satisfaction ratings. This of course ultimately affected the bottom line and it was only for this reason that he was eventually shown the door.

When taken to the worst extreme, Bullies can bring whole organizations down, or ruin the part of it for which they are responsible, simply by their intransigent attitude or unwillingness to admit that they got things wrong. Even if they are not able to influence the whole culture of an organization,

Bullies can negatively affect their peers in other ways too. They look down on those leaders who do try to fully engage with their employees by making them feel as if they are weak. Sometimes they attempt to restrict leaders beneath them from trying to apply positive leadership approaches. I once witnessed one Bully shouting "Just tell them what to ****ing do' at his deputy, because he was 'wasting time' trying to solicit ideas from the team on a task. This kind of thing frequently occurs because Bullies like to drag people down to their level. Even worse, some leaders end up emulating them in the belief that this provides the path to success. It does, in certain organizations.

Indirectly, Bullies can also have another more subtle, but equally malevolent effect on other leaders. Young and indeed mid-career executives are often unsure as to why they should bother trying to strive to become Genuine Leaders when, after all, they see these Bullies working alongside them who seem to get along just fine. Sometimes, even the head of the organization is one, as we have just seen. During the leadership programs that I deliver, I am constantly challenged by participants as to why striving to improve their capacity to lead is the best way to go. Questions invariably come in the form of: "That's all well and good, but my boss is a tyrant and, hey, he just got promoted" or "I hear what you're saying, but how come my colleague is absolutely hated by her team yet she seems to get more recognition from senior management than I do?"

Bullies may well seem to succeed, even for long periods, but sooner or later they always have a big fall in my experience. The longer they persist with the modes of behavior which earn them the title of Bully in the first place, the bigger that fall is likely to be. They might think their approach is working and unfortunately it often does for some time, but their constant destruction of relationships means that there is a very long queue of people who are only waiting to get them. Sooner or later they slip up, and when they do, Bullies quickly learn that the journey back down the leadership ladder is a fast one.

Why? Simply because they have no support mechanism left to break their fall. Take an analogy from outside of the work context. Dictators can rule countries by fear and intimidation for decades, but when they go, it is usually very quick. They are gone in a week. All it takes is a tipping point when the forces raged against them sense the time has come. The same applies to the Bullies in organizations; they usually get their comeuppance, and even if they do not, they often retire lonely and dejected characters.

Summary

Toxic Impostors, particularly the Bullies, are a stain on organizations. Yet, there is still a tendency to reward ends over means. That is because the ends are easier to measure – they are quickly seen in a budget met or from the bottom line. The damage done by the Toxic Impostors is infinitely harder to quantify and the costs associated with their behavior more difficult to calculate, but they are substantial.

There is not a leader in the world that has not lost her temper on occasion or put his own concerns in front of everything else. This again is only natural and every one of us has a bit of toxicity in us, but only a bit. The Toxic Impostors are nasty and manipulative characters by nature and, for these leaders, the potential for change is, in my experience, very limited. Why? Because their arrogance makes it very hard for them to even accept they have a problem in the first place and it is just not possible to fix something, if you do not accept that it is broken in the first place.

Make no mistake about it, though, the poor performance seen in the Impostor Leaders does not just happen by accident. Nor, to be fair, do they always act as they do on purpose, for in many cases they do not even appreciate the full effects of their behavior and actions. Intentionally or otherwise, their consistent underperformance results from a chain reaction of sorts because the Impostors lack key elements of the right stuff to lead, each of which has a knock-on effect on how they function as leaders.

The important task for you over the past chapters was to look at the various leader-types described and review your own performance considering the positive and negative behaviors described. When you spin the Leadership Wheel, which quadrant do you end up in most of the time?

The remaining chapters will explore what it is that all the Impostors lack that makes them the way they are. The content ahead revisits the key components of the right stuff and contrasts the strengths seen in the Genuine Leaders in terms of mindset, attributes, and skills against the weaknesses of the Impostors.

Notes

1 Susan Donaldson James, 'Leona Helmsley's Little Rich Dog Trouble Dies in Luxury – Wealthy Hotel Heir Left Maltese $12 Million, Ignoring Her Family in Will.' *ABC News*, online edition. June 10, 2011. https://abcnews.go.com/US/leona-helmsleys-dog-trouble-richest-world-dies-12/story?id=13810168. Accessed August 18, 2020.
2 'Leona Helmsley.' Wikipedia. Last modified August 18, 2020. https://en.wikipedia.org/wiki/Leona_Helmsley. Accessed August 18, 2020.
3 'Salvador Dalí Quotes.' www.salvadordali.com/quotes. Accessed August 18, 2020.

Chapter 6

Blinded by How They Think

People regularly get taken in by pranksters and fraudsters. On occasion, it can be in a light-hearted (albeit extremely embarrassing) way, as Prince Harry discovered.[1] He was famously hoodwinked by a telephone call from Russian pranksters that convinced him he was speaking with Greta Thunberg, the environmentalist. Throughout the call it never seemed to register with him that there was something fishy going on. He opened up to a worrying degree when he revealed he thought normality was much better than royal life. He also claimed his troubled uncle Prince Andrew was "completely separate from me and my wife." It was certainly a regrettable episode, but not devastating in the greater scheme of things. On other occasions, fraudsters can cause real and lasting pain, as anyone who was deceived by Bernard Madoff would undoubtedly testify.

Impostors of all kinds succeed because they have mastered the art of deception. Taken at face value, they might look and sound like the real McCoy, but there is usually a nasty surprise hidden behind the mask. What you see is most definitely not what you get. In Madoff's case, that deception was sustained for decades, fooling even the smartest people. But like all Impostors, his fall eventually came, and even now, many years later, the big question remains – how did so many people get taken in, for so long, for so much?

We already know that the Impostor Leaders, not unlike some pranksters and business icons, are essentially deceiving others too and that they can do so in a way that results in mild or severe consequences. Before doing so, however, some have already deceived themselves. This is perhaps the greatest failing seen in the Impostors because it lies at the heart of all their problems. When they look in the mirror, they apparently see someone completely different from what everyone else sees. They rarely recognize themselves as fakes, or fully understand the cost of their actions.

This chapter looks at how the Impostor Leaders are blinded by their low levels of self-awareness and how they make matters worse for themselves because their mindsets are wrong. It will show that they are essentially pulling the wool over their own eyes, stumbling around and repeatedly acting and behaving in ways that are counterproductive and even at times counterintuitive. They think like Impostors, so it is no surprise that they spend much of their time acting like one.

Self-Awareness Wins Every Time

Elephants are self-aware – at least, according to the findings of several research projects. In one study,[2] the researchers, using specially designed mirrors, proved that elephants can indeed recognize their own reflections, something until then it was believed that only humans, apes and to some extent dolphins could do. One of the results that surprised the researchers was just how quickly the elephants came to terms with their own image and began interacting with the mirror. They did not appear to mistake their reflections for strangers and try to greet them, as the researchers had suspected they might do. It is believed that this self-awareness contributes to the social complexity seen in elephant herds and could be linked to the empathy and concern for others in the group that they have been known to display. Even now, the researchers believe we know but a fraction about their true capacity for self-awareness.

You would really wonder though about some humans when it comes to their levels of self-awareness. Anyone who has ever watched a reality TV show will know how unaware some people are about who they are, and more importantly how they act. The behavior of some of the participants on these shows – even allowing for the editing for effect – is just beyond belief. Apart from the cringe factor, what is perhaps most amazing is that, after the event, many of them do not even realize what they did, or worse still think their behavior is somehow normal and acceptable. My money is on the elephants over some of that crowd when it comes to self-awareness, I have to say. Certainly, watching a family of elephants would be a lot more entertaining, and probably more educational, than having to sit through an episode of *Love Island*, that is for sure.

Self-awareness may not always get as much attention as some other leadership competencies, but I believe it is the most valuable in terms of raising performance. Being conscious of what he is good at, while accepting that he may still have plenty to learn pushes a leader to constantly raise the personal effectiveness bar. Unfortunately, showing any sign of weakness is still regarded as something to be avoided in many organizations when it should be viewed as a strength. Employees certainly see it in a positive light. It helps to build trust and credibility with them when they see that their leader is willing to admit they are not the perfect diamond. In terms of self-awareness, all leaders might learn a thing or two about self-analysis, and indeed humility, from former General Mills CEO Steve Sanger, who reportedly once told a gathering of his colleagues:

As you all know, last year my team told me that I needed to do a better job of coaching my direct reports. I just reviewed my 360-degree feedback. I have been working on becoming a better coach for the past year or so. I'm still not doing quite as well as I want, but I'm getting a lot better. My co-workers have been helping me improve. Another thing that I feel good about is the fact that my scores on 'effectively responds to feedback' are so high this year.[3]

People who have high levels of self-awareness are not only better off because of that fact, but it tells us something more fundamental about them. It takes honesty and real courage to admit personal failings and then to do something about them, so those who can make that journey possess the strength of character not seen in others who know themselves less well. The best performers in any field are always very self-aware.

In my experience, unlike the TV wannabees, Genuine Leaders do know themselves well and they tower over the Impostors because of it. They understand what makes them tick, recognize their strengths and weaknesses, and continuously work hard to build their capacity to lead. What I find striking about these leaders is that not only do they understand their behavior but, more importantly, they take proactive steps to manage it. It is this action orientation towards personal improvement based on their understanding of self which I believe really underpins many of their strengths as leaders. Genuine Leaders are constantly growing and improving as a result of their experiences both on and off-the-job and they derive real value from those experiences by reflecting upon and learning the lessons from what they encounter. Through regular introspection – but not of the navel-gazing kind – these leaders analyze their behavior, attitudes, and values, and take meaningful steps so that they continuously iron out their rough edges.

When I ask Genuine Leaders why they push themselves to improve, I am often met with surprised looks. It is not something they seem to consciously think about because it comes naturally to them to strive to raise their game. Often, they will say that they do so because of a belief that standing still means falling behind in an ever-changing work environment. Genuine Leaders are grounded enough to realize that the world of work is constantly evolving, and this provides the motivation for them to keep building their capabilities. They understand too that there are twin forces at play which if not responded to will quickly see them become obsolete as leaders.

On the one hand, employees' expectations of their leaders are becoming increasingly more demanding, and this trend is set to continue, and maybe even more so once we get past the COVID-19 crisis. People will have changed fundamentally because of the pandemic and this will impact on their attitudes to work, and their bosses. On the other hand, superiors too are always calling for better results from their leaders throughout the organization. To keep pace with and respond to these dual pressures, Genuine

Leaders appreciate that they must constantly push themselves. They know that staying ahead of the curve requires a real understanding of personal strengths and areas for improvement and constant attention to self-development if they are to meet the growing demands of superiors and subordinates.

By comparison, most of the Impostor Leaders that I meet seem to live in cloud-cuckoo-land most of the time and it is a major contributor to why they get so much wrong, so frequently. They only see the world from one perspective, theirs, and have a very limited or jaundiced view of themselves. This means that to varying degrees, they are often blissfully unaware of their shortcomings, or have an ability to completely ignore the signals no matter how weak or strong they may be. Even when they do recognize their failings the Impostors often seem incapable or unwilling to really address them. Here is one example of how one Impostor I encountered could not see the wood for the trees:

> After one of the many leadership courses that I have delivered to mid-career managers, one participant wrote on her feedback form: "Course was fine, but some of it was a bit too basic for me." Following up with her afterwards as part of ongoing coaching, she explained that the program lacked real impact for her as she already understood the basics. She was searching for something more "cutting edge" to reflect her needs as "someone on the fast track." Hmm.
>
> Part of her coaching program involved me sitting down with her direct report employees to explore how they viewed her skills as a leader. Initially, there was a clear reluctance from her team to collectively give an open account of work life. There was lots of, "No, everything's fine" or "She's a good boss" as they fidgeted and their eyes met the floor. But sure enough, during short individual sessions, the floodgates opened and quite a few in her team were very disillusioned by her. Yes, things had started brightly enough when she first took over two years previously, and initially she seemed like a great leader, but in the words of one of her team "she only looks out for herself. We are not really that important unless she wants something." The general theme was one of feeling undervalued and unimportant to her and that she could be quite condescending and sarcastic at times with people, particularly if they messed up.
>
> There was regular communication, annual appraisals, and even team outings happening, so on paper she was doing many of the right things. But as another employee put it when referring to communicating with her, "It all goes in one ear and out the other. Nothing ever changes."

This is far from an isolated scenario of poor self-awareness among Impostors in my experience. Here was a pure Egotist, who refused to even question her approach, even though structured feedback had highlighted similar issues for her many times previously. In giving her this feedback, which was received with only mildly concealed disdain I might add, it was clear that indeed it was all going in one ear and out the other. Ultimately, it is true that you cannot save some people from themselves. Self-confidence is a good thing, self-delusion is not.

Opening the Window to Self

Genuine Leaders understand the importance of structured and constructive feedback in guiding their efforts to get better at what they do, so they constantly search out opportunities to build their self-awareness. They understand that getting the views of others whom they know and trust is vital in order to have a truly rounded picture of their own performance. Over time, Genuine Leaders build up a very clear picture of where their areas for improvement lie and they then take concerted action to play to their strengths and minimize the negative impacts of their weaknesses. What I have found is that the ability of these leaders to be open with others also helps them build and sustain deeper relationships which have value and meaning for both parties.

Impostor Leaders, as we have just seen, tend to run a mile from feedback or at best they are only begrudgingly open to it. When forced to endure it, they usually let it wash over them like our 'fast track' friend, without really taking the valid messages on board. Nor, in my experience, do the Impostors have anything like the same capacity to be open with others as Genuine Leaders do. As a result, they end up knowing little about themselves and with time they tend to get worse not better as managers.

As an aside, although the Impostors will rarely disclose information about themselves, I find them to be quite cunning at the same time, because they are usually very eager to find out as much as they can about other people even in some cases using underhanded methods. They do so, not as a bridge builder, but often they believe that the more they know about a person, the more power they can potentially wield over them.

When Impostors do become aware that they are essentially closed to the outside world, many are often happy to stay in their dark, unenlightened world caring little about how others view them or ignoring the consequences of their poor self-awareness. Frequently, and you may have noticed this, they will blame others for the problems too, as in the Bully who, having upset an employee puts it down to that person being too weak or soft as opposed to any fault of their own. What all Impostor Leaders fail to realize is that it is themselves who suffer in the long run if they do not first raise their self-awareness and then more critically do something to work on their weak areas.

Mindset Matters

Would you reply to the following job advert?

> Men wanted for hazardous journey, small wages, bitter cold, long months of complete darkness, constant danger, safe return doubtful, honor and recognition in case of success.[4]

In 1914 over five thousand men did reply. Twenty-seven of them were selected and in August that year, they set off from England under the command of Sir Ernest Shackleton[5] on an Antarctic expedition with the intention of being the first to complete a transcontinental crossing. From the moment their ship *Endurance* entered the Weddell Sea, off the Antarctic Peninsula, in early 1915 anything that could possibly have gone wrong with the mission did go wrong. *Endurance* became trapped in ice and was later crushed by its force and they remained stranded for months on ice flows suffering one unimaginable challenge after the other, including having to undertake a seven-day sea voyage in flimsy lifeboats to reach the uninhabited Elephant Island which still lay beyond the possibility of rescue.

Yet, despite the hopelessness of their position, Shackleton's optimism never waned during the endless months of uncertainty. Staring death in the face, he still did not quit. As a last throw of the dice, he and several crew members undertook a treacherous voyage in a small boat, crossing 800 miles of the roughest seas on earth in order to reach the nearest inhabited island, South Georgia; a feat later described without hyperbole as the equivalent of finding a needle in a haystack. Then, having landed on the wrong side of that island, they had to cross over the uncharted mountainous interior to reach the whaling station, from where rescue for his remaining men would later be launched. He had promised them he would return and return he did on August 30, 1916. Not one member of the party was lost.

The story of Shackleton's legendary Antarctic expedition has become a popular lesson in leadership in recent years, and it is, for me, one of the greatest stories of human survival ever told. Shackleton undoubtedly had many great qualities as a leader, but he himself placed optimism at the top of the list of attributes that saw him through the ordeal, followed by patience, and imagination. As he said himself, "difficulties are just things to overcome, after all." Without this mindset, it is probable that he and all his men would have met a cold and painful death.

Leaders in the workplace do not, thankfully, have to face such a series of seemingly insurmountable challenges, but mindset still matters for every one of them, even if the scale of what they face every day pales into insignificance in comparison to what Shackleton had to endure. Genuine Leaders always have an upbeat and determined outlook which contributes to their ability to lead. Impostors tend to have the opposite and their mindset is another personal feature which keeps them at the back of the leadership class. They fail to recognize that the path to becoming the best at anything lies as much in how they think as it does in what they do.

In my dealings with Genuine Leaders, I find that they tend to look at life in a very positive way. No, they do not come running across the car park every morning waving their arms in the air chanting some uplifting mantra, nor do they wear tee-shirts with Carpe Diem written on it. But, by nature, they are optimists who recognize that the potential for success or failure in life is largely in their own hands. There is a refreshing and uplifting aspect to how Genuine Leaders view the world; they intuitively understand the laws of attraction. They know that how they think will directly influence how far they can go in life and that their inner attitude will attract like-minded individuals to them.

When it comes specifically to the leadership role, my interactions with Genuine Leaders also tell me that they have a unique view of what leading others entails today. As a start point, these leaders seem to constantly strive to reduce overall levels of negativity in the workplace because they know that when negativity increases, productivity and quality tend to decline. Genuine Leaders think very differently about how they lead others, which in turn influences how they act, as summarized in Figure 6.1.

Genuine Leaders stand out because they:	
Think Differently	*Act Differently*
Recognize that attitudes to work today are radically different	Apply innovative approaches to bring the best out of people
Understand that just telling employees what to do might seem easier but it doesn't get the best results over the long term	Involve employees in decision making when appropriate and regularly utilise two-way communication channels
Realize that it is the people who ultimately achieve business outcomes	Strive to engage their team, not just occasionally but all the time
Accept that people are all different and as such will not all act in the same way or respond to the same approach	Develop their relationship management skills to a high level and have flexibility in their approach
Acknowledge that the past cannot be changed, only learned from and continuously look to the future	Have a clear view of where they are going which they continuously communicate to their team
Understand that the days of "do as I say, not what I do" are long gone	Are role models for those around them – not perfect or infallible by any means – but continuously striving to be better

Figure 6.1 Genuine Leaders Think Differently

Ken Blanchard, the respected leadership expert and author, described the mindset of Genuine Leaders well when he said: "In the past, a leader was a boss. Today's leaders must be partners with their people, they can no longer lead solely based on positional power."[6] This principle drives Genuine Leaders to build and sustain bonds with their employees, not out of any weakness, but because they are strong and I have seen time and time again how these leaders recognize that without the commitment and support of their people, seeking to achieve organizational goals remains a wish, not a probability.

Self-Incarceration

Few people would argue that many of the fraudsters you hear about in real life deserve to end up in jail. Just like Bernie Madoff did. For the Impostor Leaders, imprisoning them would undoubtedly be an extreme measure, although I have met many employees over the years that would gladly have done so with their boss and happily thrown away the key too. In any case, the Impostors do not need to be locked away because they are already imprisoned. It is a form of self-incarceration. They are trapped in their own personal prisons because their mindsets are wrong.

When you get to know Impostors, you find that they are all con-strained by their outlook on life. Of course, they are not all manic depressives or Moaning Minnies, but they do have self-limiting perspec-tives in terms of how they view the world which naturally influences how they behave:

- Most of the Deflating Impostors that I have met generally view the world with a degree of trepidation and/or negativity. They seem to consider outside forces as having the power to determine the direction they take rather than being truly in control of their own destinies.
- The mindset of Toxic Impostors is complex for sure, but often quite sad in some ways. In my experience, many of these characters, particularly the Bullies, feel a sense of isolation which gets progressively worse over time because their behavior causes them to be further isolated. It is self-perpetuating in many ways. Often, they are running from something too without ever being fully sure what that is and the barriers they put up around them are in fact a form of self-preservation.

In relation to how they view the leadership role, the Impostor Leaders suffer from common mental blocks. Clearly, they do not all think alike in this regard either, but they do show some uniform flaws which impact on how they perform. While Genuine Leaders accept the three dimensions of work (People, Process, and Performance) and the engage-achieve relation-ship, to one extent or another, the Impostors do not. I have to say that this is not because they are stupid, but it does not seem to fully register with them to the extent that it really serves to guide their behavior. The Deflating Impostors, either through insecurity or disinterest seem not to understand the equation at all. The Toxic Impostors only see one side of it: outcomes. To them that is all that matters because they fail to realize that over the long term the quality of one part of the equation influences the other.

What I find to be one of the biggest contrasts from Genuine Leaders is how all the Impostors tend to see their position as being the primary source of their power and authority. As long as they have the title, they seem to believe that others must act in accordance with their wishes. Unfortunately, this is already a very outdated mindset and will become even more so in future. The upcoming generation just do not buy it, nobody does. But the fact that the Imposters think this way reduces the motivation for them to adapt to changing circumstances. In fact, talk to most of them and they believe that it is up to their employees to adapt to their style, not the other way around.

The idea that mindset matters is certainly not new, but it is becoming much clearer as to how much it does matter in terms of performance and achievement. How a leader thinks sets the context for everything they do and in the case of the Genuine Leaders, their ability to succeed in the role comes initially from the fact that, for them, nothing within reason is impossible. Impostors are who they are largely because they believe that the possibilities are always limited.

Summary

Genuine Leaders tend to learn and grow from their experiences. Impostors continuously miss these opportunities and, unfortunately, it is not just the immediate problems that this causes which should concern them. Poor self-awareness and negativity tend to get progressively worse, so unless they radically change and begin to take proactive steps to better themselves, Impostors get stuck in their limited leadership style. Sadly, the way they think not only contributes to their current predicament but makes it infinitely more difficult for them to take the wool from their eyes.

The Genuine Leaders also differ fundamentally from Impostors in how they view life generally and particularly in how they see the leadership role. Impostors have constraining mindsets and again they seem to miss the point that it is themselves who suffer because of this. Their thought processes are wrong, so it is probably not that much of a shock that they frequently act in self-defeating ways.

The following chapter explores how the Impostors are further constrained because they lack certain attributes which are proven to underpin effective leadership.

Notes

1 'Prince Harry "Duped by Greta Thunberg Call" Russian Pranksters Say.' BBC News, online edition. March 11, 2020. www.bbc.com/news/uk-51831374. Accessed August 18, 2020.

2 Charles Q. Choi, 'Elephant Self-Awareness Mirrors Humans.' Live Science. October 30, 2006. www.livescience.com/4272-elephant-awareness-mirrors-humans.html. Accessed August 18, 2020.

3 Marshall Goldsmith, 'To Help Others Develop, Start with Yourself.' Fast Company. January 1, 2004. www.fastcompany.com/48377/help-others-develop-start-yourself. Accessed August 18, 2020.

4 Joshua Horn, 'Shackleton's Ad – Men Wanted for Hazardous Journey.' Discerning History. May 15, 2013. http://discerninghistory.com/2013/05/shackletons-ad-men-wanted-for-hazerdous-journey. Accessed August 18, 2020.

5 'Ernest Shackleton.' Wikipedia. Last modified July 17, 2020. https://en.wikipedia.org/wiki/Ernest_Shackleton. Accessed August 18, 2020.

6 BrainyQuote. www.brainyquote.com/quotes/ken_blanchard_173324. Accessed August 18, 2020.

Chapter 7

Constrained by Who They Are

Maybe I need to get out more often, but I find it very interesting to consider why some people succeed whereas others do not, even when similarly talented. In any walk of life, talent alone is never the sole differentiator between those who excel and others who fail to reach the same heights. Nothing highlights this quite as well as a reported encounter between John Daly, that talented but wayward golfer, and Tiger Woods, the most successful golfer of the modern era. Apparently at one tournament, Daly was sitting enjoying a beer with friends when Tiger passed the table on his way to the gym. Daly shouted across to Tiger asking him whether he never got tired of exercising and invited him to join them for a drink. Tiger quipped back, "If I had your talent, I wouldn't need to exercise."[1]

I am no golfer, but I can tell you that Tiger Woods has not achieved all that he has done on the golf course purely because of his high skill levels and scratch handicap. Many in the know argue that John Daly has at times shown equal flair with the golf club. What he seemed to lack was the drive and determination that made Tiger such a special player, which is best captured in his own words, "I love to play golf, and that's my arena. And you can characterize it and describe it however you want, but I have a love and a passion for getting that ball in the hole and beating those guys." We now know that Tiger had other passions too, as past events have shown, yet he still had the right stuff to make it as a top golfer – and to make a comeback after many years in the wilderness. John Daly, on the other hand, came up a bit short in that regard. Being consistently the best at anything requires more than just talent or skill and this applies not only in golfing circles but in all areas of life, including leadership.

Now Tiger's personal reputation took a battering some years back and whatever the rights and wrongs of it all, his actions simply proved to me that the man is human. The way he fought to pick up the pieces of his life since then, and overcame the trauma of multiple back operations, tells us a lot too about the man. Despite all the damage done to his image, what he has, and continues, to achieve on the golf course still holds positive lessons which can be applied in a leadership context, namely that talent on its own is never a guarantee of success. Coming back to win the US Masters in 2019 was simply breathtaking.

Impostor Leaders have high internal handicaps because they are further constrained by who they are, and this adds to the reasons why they struggle in the role. This chapter builds on the previous and looks at how the Impostors underachieve, when compared to Genuine Leaders, in large part because they are missing certain personal characteristics that form a vital part of the right stuff to lead.

Characteristically Good

There are many personal qualities that underpin success in a leadership role and Genuine Leaders always have them in abundance, which further helps to give them the edge over the Impostors. The range of attributes that can help raise leadership performance is certainly very broad and there is no ideal list. However, I have seen certain qualities time and time again in the best leaders that I have met and the engage-achieve dynamic can help to pinpoint what they are (see Figure 7.1). These traits in the diagram are not intended to be an exhaustive list, but in my experience Genuine Leaders always have a good mix of these characteristics.

Before moving on, this list raises an important concern which is worth side-tracking on for a moment. One question that frequently arises (and we have mentioned it many times already) is whether charisma is a pre-requisite for Genuine Leaders. Naturally, some degree of charisma – whatever that is, for it is somewhat intangible – is a great quality to have as a leader once as said before it is not mistaken for something else. Every Genuine Leader that I have met was charismatic to some extent, but with the exception of Stars that does not mean they were all shining lights. Sure, they were mostly extroverts, but it is a mistake to think that only those very few individuals who ooze charisma can ever hope to become Genuine Leaders. Were that the case, the potential pool of candidates would be very small indeed. Yes, having charisma helps for certain but it is also possible to engage and inspire others through strength of character or indeed intellectual prowess.

In any case, it is not all upside when it relates to charisma and too much of it can be as bad as having none. Like many things in life, charisma is good in moderation and some level of it is undoubtedly a plus but not necessarily a must have for all Genuine Leaders. That is why it is not on our list. One thing for certain though is that the Impostors do not have it, or when they think they do, it is because they believe charisma and arrogance to be in the same family when in reality they are not even distantly related.

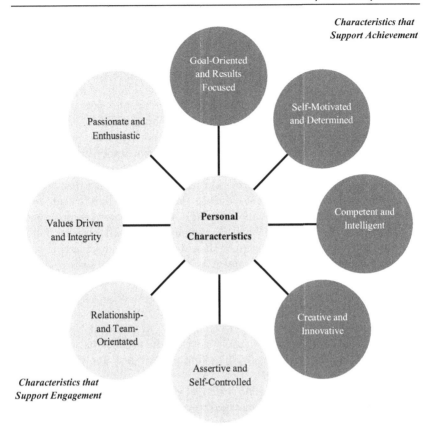

Figure 7.1 Common Characteristics of Genuine Leaders

Characteristics that Support Engagement

Genuine Leaders have a head start in the race to effectiveness because from what I have seen they always have strengths across a combination of characteristics which result in them having high emotional intelligence. The ability to really bond with others as a leader is not only about having good communication skills or flexible leadership styles, although these are vital. Without the right characteristics these skills are of little value because it is the personal qualities that help the skills to 'stick,' as this little encounter proved to me:

Some time back I was working with an organization that had several business units in different city-center locations. These units had similar offerings, mainly directed at the corporate market, and operated under comparable economic and competitive conditions. In general, the performance of all the units was living up to expectations, except for one.

In working with the general manager to identify ways to improve things at the underperforming unit, the issue of leadership naturally arose. During our discussions, he made a comment which was blunt, but telling: "Look, these people are paid to do a job and I expect them to do what they are paid to do. If they don't like it, then they know where the door is." The reference to 'these people' says it all really. This comment was a snapshot of his overall approach, and no prizes for guessing that the problems at this unit were not resource, marketing, or product related, they were a direct result of poor leadership.

Some of his employees described their reactions to his frequent outbursts as 'riding out the storm' and they readily admitted that when he lost it with them, they just stood there and waited for him to calm down. One or two of his more senior staff, the stronger characters, described it differently. They called it 'kangaroo boxing' (do not ask me why, but the fact that this manager was Australian might have had something to do with it). Anyway, what they meant by this was that they gave as good as they got, and heated arguments and battles regularly ensued.

This Impostor Leader, a real Bully, was given lots of support and coaching by his superiors to help him improve, and they even signed him up for a prestigious leadership course where he covered the usual skills such as how to communicate more effectively, handling conflict and applying different leadership styles.

But our Australian friend found little real value from the program back at work. Why? Because he never managed to control his temper, so he was not able to put the new skills into practice in any meaningful way. To be fair, he did try to become a better communicator, but every time he found himself under pressure or stressed he reverted to type, quickly losing his cool, with the result that all the learning went out the window. It became clear that he did not have the right personal qualities, like self-control, to give him the ability to apply the skills. It is for this reason that emotional intelligence matters because relationship management skills are only truly of value when the foundation is right.

Assertive and Self-Controlled

Daily life in any work environment can be akin to a pressure cooker at times and every leader regularly faces all sorts of emotional triggers which can send them into orbit if they are not assertive and able to maintain high levels of self-control. In particular, dealing with people can be very frustrating at times and I have yet to find an organization where there was not one or two individuals floating around who could push even the calmest leader to the limit, like this guy once reported in an article from the *Daily Telegraph* in the UK:

CARETAKER WHO FELL OFF STEPLADDER SUES FOR £50,000
OVER 'INADEQUATE TRAINING'
A school caretaker who was injured falling off a six-foot stepladder is
suing his employer for £50,000 claiming he was not trained how to use
it properly. The caretaker claimed that his bosses did not show him
how to use the 6ft ladder safely, although he admits using others for at
least 30 years without mishap.

The caretaker told the court he had signed a form to say he had
received 'ladder training' but said this only consisted of being warned
not to stand on the top platform or work at higher than three metres off
the ground. "I thought that was the extent of ladder training," he told
the court. "I didn't know there were other things regarding ladders."[2]

Now, it would be more than a little tempting to hit him with the ladder, I
fear, but Genuine Leaders would suppress that urge. Even when faced with
those few employees, colleagues, or situations which really test their
patience the noticeable thing about these leaders is how they can remain in
control. They might well boil up inside, but they can manage their responses
because they are assertive characters who are on top of their emotions.
When they do lose their temper, and like everyone that happens from time
to time, they do so not through impulse but more likely out of choice,
because they feel that a bit of a wake-up call is required. This ability to be
assertive, linked to self-confidence, influences everything they do but particularly helps them as communicators or when responding to the variety of
triggers they encounter every day and because of that, I find that employees
frequently describe Genuine Leaders as being 'calm and in control.'

Impostor Leaders, on the other hand, are never assertive enough and it
creates a lot of headaches for them. The Deflating Impostors are usually too
passive or anxious, which in the case of Damp Squibs, causes them to be
over controlling of their people, or for Dark Clouds means they flounder
helplessly in the role. For both sets of Deflating Impostors, their lack of
assertiveness means they often fail to tackle problems head-on and that is
why I mentioned earlier that they frequently end up manipulating events
from behind the scenes.

Given half a chance, some of the Toxic Impostors I know would most
definitely use the ladder as a weapon. Both the Egotists and Bullies often
delude themselves that they are assertive characters, but they are most certainly not. What they frequently are in my experience is aggressive, although
as highlighted they may apply that aggression in different ways. Egotists are
mostly covert aggressors whereas Bullies act like a bull in a china shop,
frequently trampling all over the rights of others, discounting their views, or
damaging their self-esteem.

By managing their reactions to events, Genuine Leaders can think first,
and then act whereas the Impostors, and particularly the Bullies, do the

opposite. It is not unusual either to find them regretting what they have said or done once they have regained control. Without assertiveness and self-control, the Impostors unfortunately become prisoners of their emotions which naturally cause them to be more erratic and less effective.

Relationship- and Team-Orientated

Being relationship and team-oriented are such obvious cornerstones of effective leadership that it may seem somewhat unnecessary to have to highlight these qualities here. Yet, even though it is well known that these characteristics add greatly to a leader's ability to engage others, many Impostors seem clueless as to where other people are coming from or show a complete lack of concern for others. This is not an exaggeration and, worse still, I have frequently watched in shock at how some of them have a perverted sense of how to get the best out of their employees.

Genuine Leaders have an innate ability to be aware of, and sensitive to, the emotions and feelings of others. When these leaders say things like "I understand where you are coming from," they really mean it, and Bob Galvin, former CEO of Motorola, got it right about the importance of empathy when referring to his father, the founder of the company:

> Dad once looked down at the assembly line of women and thought: "These are all like my own mom – they have kids, homes to take care of, people who need them." It motivated him to work hard because he saw his own mom in all of them. That's how it all begins – with respect and empathy.[3]

Having this ability to empathize not only allows Genuine Leaders to strengthen their ties with people but it also helps them to understand what style of leadership will work best in any given situation. Closely in tune with human nature, they are far more effective because of that and have a natural tendency to build positive relationships with others. Genuine Leaders are team orientated by nature, thinking in terms of teams and not just groups of people, with the result that they show a real concern for their employees' levels of motivation. They monitor it, notice if it is out of sync, find out why, and deal with any blockages. That does not mean that they are soft touches though, because they can quickly tell when someone is trying to pull a fast one too.

Both the Deflating and Toxic Impostors have lower empathy levels which means they tend to act in a way that fulfils their own needs first, regardless of whether it addresses, or is even cognizant of the legitimate needs and feelings of others. Particularly for the Bullies, this lack of empathy is what makes them capable of inflicting emotional distress on others without seeming to feel any remorse. Some studies have even shown that ultra-bullies take this lack of empathy to the extreme – showing an absence of empathy comparable to those seen in the worst sociopaths. Monty Burns, that boss from hell in *The Simpsons*, used to welcome his employees to the start of a new week with such memorable quotes as, "Monday morning. Time to pay for your two days of debauchery, you hungover drones."[4] No doubt for some of the Bullies I have had the misfortune to run into, this represents a pretty accurate description of how they saw their people.

The aloof or negative side to Deflating Impostors also means that they are usually very poor relationship builders and they tend not to be all that team-orientated as a result. Particularly, I find that the Damp Squibs prefer to deal with employees on an individual basis because they feel more comfortable in maintaining control that way. Toxic Impostors – well being honest – they are relationship and team destroyers most of the time.

Values Driven and Integrity

"I remember landing under sniper fire. There was supposed to be some kind of a greeting ceremony at the airport, but instead we just ran with our heads down to get into the vehicles to get to our base."[5] Getting slightly carried away on the campaign trail for the presidency a few years ago, Hillary Clinton used this reference to a trip she took as First Lady to Bosnia in 1996 in order to prove her battle-hardened experience. Turns out, it was a bit of an exaggeration and her arrival had been somewhat less dramatic.

The reality was, as old news video footage of the event later confirmed, that she had arrived without incident, accompanied by her then 15-year-old daughter Chelsea, the comedian Sinbad and singer Sheryl Crow. I thought Sinbad's comments were funny when he later said that Hillary's description of what actually went on was ridiculous: "What kind of President would say, 'Hey, man, I can't go 'cause I might get shot so I'm going to send my wife ... oh ... and take a guitar player and a comedian with you.'" Her advisors later admitted she 'misspoke' about the incident.

Just like Hillary, we all misspeak on occasion. In fact, research shows that each one of us is prone to uttering the odd white lie every now and again. At that level, it is not a sign of a lack of values or integrity but has more to do with our collective propensity towards exaggeration. The white lie issue reminds me of a charming – if very old story – story about Lillian Carter, the mother of President Carter, or Miss Lillian as she was affectionately known at the time. On one occasion a reporter asked her whether it was true that her son never lied. She replied, "Well, I reckon he might have told a little white lie now and then."[6] Seizing on what he thought was an opportunity for a big story – the president lied and what not – the reporter followed up by saying that she had previously said her son never lied and asking her what she actually meant by a 'white lie.' "Well," replied Miss Lillian, "do you remember when you came in this morning and I told you how nice you looked and how glad I was to see you?"

Telling the odd little porky is one thing but lacking values and integrity is quite another matter entirely. While we will all make allowances for the occasional massaging of the truth, an absence of values or lack of integrity is never acceptable in our leaders, be they on the political stage or in the workplace.

Genuine Leaders are always values-driven individuals who have high levels of integrity. I would not like to give the impression that they are all some sort of clones of Pope Francis, but from what I have seen, their deeply held personal principles do seem to serve as beacons for them, guiding their actions and informing all their decisions. It is this sense of values which drives them to seek proactive co-operation in their dealings with others, both in and outside the organization. They recognize the importance of ethical behavior and demonstrate their values through their leadership style and actions. Clearly, they may not like all their employees to the same degree, but in dealing with them every day their belief in natural justice means that they strive to treat them all equally and fairly.

Genuine Leaders never blatantly mislead their people either and as they do view their employees as partners, it comes naturally for them to be open and honest with their team members. Even when they cannot give their employees the full story, these leaders are at least honest as to why. Their people may not like the answer, but they respect the honesty.

It would be very wrong to say that all Impostors lack values but in the case of the Deflating Impostors I find they tend not to shine through as clearly in their actions. They do of course hold particular beliefs, but they are often willing to compromise them in order to 'go with the flow' or, worse still, simply when it is personally beneficial for them to do so. They are, however, mostly fair to their employees, spreading the control or doom and gloom equally to everyone. Deflating Impostors, to one extent or another, also tend to run their operations something akin to the CIA – far too much is based on a secretive rather than an open and collaborative approach. Toxic Impostors do not for the most part have any real sense of values, for if they did they could not act the way they do, and they most definitely do not treat all their people fairly. Nor are they the most honest individuals on the planet, and often they are just liars. Harsh perhaps, but frequently true in my experience.

Passionate and Enthusiastic

The late Steve Jobs, of Apple fame, was a great man for quotes. He once said: "Your work is going to fill a large part of your life, and the only way to be truly satisfied is to do what you believe is great work. And the only way to do great work is to love what you do."[7] Although some of his employees might argue that he did not always practice what he preached in terms of leadership style, the point Jobs makes remains valid. Genuine Leaders are 'up' most of the time because they love what they do. From what I can gather they are doing what they do, not solely because it pays the bills, but because it truly fulfils them. These leaders simply make people feel good about being around them because they are passionate people and this serves to lift and inspire those close to them. Their enthusiastic nature is infectious and spreads to others.

The Deflating Impostors are akin to emotional black holes. Rather than spreading passion and enthusiasm, they tend to suck it up. In that sense, I like to refer to them as work life's vampires. Try as they might, Damp Squibs only succeed in radiating about as much passion and enthusiasm as a small candle, whereas the Dark Clouds, well, they just block out the light. The Toxic Impostors might appear quite passionate, but there is often something a bit too manic about them at times. Particularly in relation to Bullies, there is certainly energy there, but it feels something like sitting beside a ticking time bomb waiting for it to go off. It is a negative force rather than something which serves to uplift.

The collective impact of these four Engaging Characteristics serves to draw people towards Genuine Leaders. Their absence in the Impostors only serves to drive them away. An interesting episode from a workshop that I once held particularly demonstrates why such qualities are so essential to the leadership role:

> During an ideas session on how to improve business performance in the organization, one talented, but extremely de-motivated employee, surprisingly suggested several positive things which would make a difference. When later asked why he had not previously told his boss about these ideas, his response was blunt but fairly revealing: "I don't get paid from the neck up."

It was certainly one of the better quips that I have heard in all my time spent dealing with employees. Here was a guy who was so disengaged that he saw his role as being to do, but not to think. You might wonder why he stayed or even why he was allowed to, but the fact was he was there and was not contributing as much as he could to the business. What it does highlight though is how being emotionally 'in tune' with others helps Genuine Leaders to stand out. An employee would never be allowed to fall to this level of disengagement under an effective leader.

Whatever leadership is or is not concerned with, it is certainly about dealing with the neck up part of the human being. It is from the neck up where employees have the potential to add value to an organization. If it was only about the neck down, then robots could easily replace people and we would not need to worry about leadership. Genuine Leaders always have great ability to deal with people from the neck up. Their personal qualities help them to understand and respond to the attitudes, emotions, and behaviors of others. Alternatively, the Impostors as a rule never have the same levels of emotional intelligence.

Characteristics that Support Achievement

On the achievement side, Genuine Leaders have certain attributes that optimize their ability to get things done and deliver outstanding results. Impostors again lack some or all of these qualities which naturally reduces their capacity for achieving the best results possible.

Goal-Orientation and Results-Focused

In 1962, J. F. Kennedy said in a speech at Rice University: "We choose to go to the moon in this decade and do the other things, not because they are easy, but because they are hard ..."[8] In saying this, he is credited with setting a target that lifted the aspirations of a generation and energized a nation. To this day, the concept of proactive goal setting and focusing on desired results is promoted as a prerequisite for individual and organizational success. They are, but with some reservations attached, in my opinion.

Goals are good, if the goals are good. What I mean by this is that setting unrealistic goals, be they personal or organizational, can do more harm than good. Too many people today, driven by a lot of quick fix self-help psychobabble – or the find success overnight with the law of attraction nonsense – set improbable goals for themselves given their talents and the level of effort they are prepared to put into realizing them. This can, when those goals are not achieved, have a negative rather than a positive impact. Organizations too must be careful when setting goals in terms of how they are devised and structured because badly designed goals can be worse than having no goals at all, for they can lead everyone in a direction that is counterproductive. I have seen many organizations establish goals, for example in terms of revenue, which although achieved were not of utmost value because the costs generated in making those revenue targets meant the increased revenue did not proportionally translate to the bottom line.

Goal orientation and Genuine Leaders go hand in hand, but with these provisions in mind. First and foremost, these leaders are good at setting realistic personal goals, which stretch them for sure, but are also within their capability to realize. They never fall into the trap of believing that any goal is achievable just because it is set. In a work context, these leaders always have a clear view of what they are trying to achieve, but they make sure that these goals have the effect of adding real value to the organization.

In tackling the goal issue, I have noticed how Genuine Leaders have the knack of making the goals more tangible and meaningful for their people and they always seem to try to:

- Include their people in defining the goals in the first place, where possible.
- Break long-term goals into shorter focused sub-goals. This helps them to identify 'little wins' which encourage further effort.
- Get everyone to publicly commit to attaining the goals. Breaking promises is not something most people like to do.
- Offer ongoing encouragement and motivate their employees to keep going.
- Allow their people to self-monitor progress. Ownership is everything.
- Provide continuous feedback on that progress.
- Recognize and address blockages which may be holding things back.

Once business goals are set, Genuine Leaders are great at building and sustaining buy in for them, so much so that I have often been quite surprised at just how much employees come to see the goals as being their own. This has the result that those who work for these leaders tend to feel part of something bigger than themselves and view the achievement of organizational goals and satisfying their own needs and aspirations as being compatible, not contradictory.

Deflating Impostors tend to have lower goal horizons in general and always struggle to harness enthusiasm from others towards them. For Damp Squibs, goals are often only set at a level in line with expectations, while for Dark Clouds they are more likely to follow whatever goals are set for them as opposed to establishing their own. Toxic Impostors naturally have goals too, but they tend to be personal first, then organizational. Where they see themselves going takes precedence, particularly for Egotists. These leaders, I have found, rarely think in terms of common goals which have the support of employees.

Self-Motivated and Determined

You may already have heard about Aron Ralston's story, or seen the movie *127 Hours*.[9] For those that have not, here in a nutshell is what happened.

One fine day in May 2003, Aron set off on what he expected would be an enjoyable hike through the mountains in Utah. How wrong he was. Very quickly, the trip turned into his, and indeed anyone's, worst nightmare. Following an accident, his arm became trapped behind an 800-pound boulder. He was stuck. Badly hurt. And in the middle of nowhere. Worse still, nobody knew he had gone on the trip – he had committed the mortal sin in mountaineering terms of not telling anyone where he was going – and he had no means of communication, so rescue was unlikely.

After five days alone, trapped and in pain, he was forced to take an unimaginable decision in order to survive. He used his pocket-knife to amputate his arm and free himself from the boulder. Yes, I did say pocket-knife. He later said that he did not lose his hand but gained his life back. Serious determination, that is for sure.

Determination is certainly an important trait to have, and never more so than during these crazy times. In fact, when you really think about it, in all walks of life little is achieved without the ability to keep going, no matter what the odds. But could you have hacked part of your own arm off with a pocket-knife, even if your survival was at stake? I am not so sure whether I could have done that; probably I would have, but you never know what you are made of until you find yourself in such a position.

Fortunately, Genuine Leaders do not have to lose an arm to succeed. Nonetheless, they are always very self–motivated and determined individuals who recognise that having personal and organizational goals is all well and good but achieving them is another matter entirely. They seem to live by a philosophy best described by Andrew Carnegie the American industrialist, who once said: "People who are unable to motivate themselves must be content with mediocrity, no matter how impressive their other talents."[10] Genuine Leaders embody this belief and can drive themselves forward, never giving up regardless of the obstacles they face. This trait, coupled with their positive attitude, can help them to proactively confront all difficult situations and gives others a sense of confidence and comfort. That, for me at least, is a big part of the reason why they tend to get better results. For sure, like all people, there are days when they feel like being somewhere else, but they can raise their game even when they do not really feel up to it.

Deflating Impostors have low levels of both these qualities in my experience. Damp Squibs are largely motivated by the fear of failure or the desire not to be seen to lag behind their peers. They may be determined, but it comes across in the wrong way because it is seen more as a desire not to get things wrong or to be shown up. Dark Clouds are motivated by the clock and are mainly determined not to be found out. Both types of Toxic Impostors are self-motivated, but not in the right sense. As we mentioned many times now, they only see the 'self' bit and their determination is often focused on getting them where they want to go personally, as opposed to seeing the bigger picture.

Competent and Intelligent

Being competent and intelligent is obviously an important leadership characteristic but this does not necessarily mean that Genuine Leaders are always the brightest people in the building. Concerns about the contribution of intelligence to leadership effectiveness have been debated for a long time. Is having a massive intellect a prerequisite to making it as a Genuine Leader?

It is pretty much accepted that having the highest IQ is not a guarantee of success. Potentially it can be a deterrent, because those with very high IQ scores can tend to have low emotional intelligence. Yet, it is unlikely that the dumbest person around is going to make it as a Genuine Leader either.

The Genuine Leaders that I encounter are always bright characters who benefit from having different forms of intelligence: the capacity to analyze and solve problems, knowledge related to the requirements of their job, or an ability to be creative. Added to that, they always had a fair helping of that critical, if somewhat intangible commodity, called common sense.

Impostors are not, for the most part at least, the village idiots. When you talk with them they are often competent and intelligent individuals. After all, total incompetence or stupidity would not be accepted. Damp Squibs are frequently highly intelligent, but they generally lack street smarts or, as highlighted, emotional intelligence. Dark Clouds though are, in my experience, usually of average intelligence and sail close to the wind when it comes to the incompetence tag. Egotists too can be quite intelligent and competent but never to the degree that they believe. Certainly, they have convinced themselves that they are a cut above everyone else in the brains department. Yes, their heads are bigger, but whether there is as much going on inside as they would like to think is a matter which is more than open to debate. Bullies are rarely the sharpest tool in the box, and I think that their nasty behaviors are often designed to mask that fact.

Creative and Innovative

Genuine Leaders also seem to have a strong aptitude for innovation and are adept at finding creative solutions to problems which arise. They are not afraid to try new things, yet that does not necessarily mean that they always have the answers themselves; due to the environment they create, ideas and suggestions come frequently from their people. They encourage the flow of innovation in the organization.

When it comes to creativity Deflating Impostors tend not to be very innovative either, particularly where significant change is required as anything too radical would represent high risk, so the tried and tested with maybe slight modifications is usually the preferred choice. Particularly, Damp Squibs will be the ones you will hear saying things like "we need to think outside the box on this one," but the very act of using such a phrase is a likely sign of lack of creativity in itself. Dark Clouds do not do creativity. Toxic Impostors limit their ability to create new ideas because they shut off one of the most important channels – their employees. I have frequently seen them rob ideas rather than create new ones of their own.

Having the right mix of these achieving characteristics helps Genuine Leaders to map out the direction they want to go in. It also enables them to consistently focus their efforts on realizing the defined goals. The Impostors are not completely lacking in all these qualities, but they do not have the same degree of strengths. Overall, from what I have seen they do tend to be stronger in the achieving rather than the engaging characteristics but unfortunately this is comparable to having only one wheel on a bike. Both are needed.

Summary

Genuine Leaders are not perfect beings that excel in every way, and there is no intention to portray them as such. However, they do have talents across a broad range of characteristics which build their capacity to both engage and achieve. Impostor Leaders are frequently constrained in how they perform because when it comes to this important element of the right stuff to lead they are at a major disadvantage, so it is no wonder they struggle. The words of Dee Hock, founder and former CEO of Visa, are a good guide as to what all the Impostors need to start doing more of:

> Here is the very heart and soul of the matter. If you look to lead, invest at least 40% of your time managing yourself – your ethics, character, principles, purpose, motivation, and conduct. Invest at least 30% managing those with authority over you, and 15% managing your peers. Use the remainder to induce those you 'work for' to understand and practice the theory. I use the terms 'work for' advisedly, for if you don't understand that you should be working for your mislabeled 'subordinates,' you haven't understood anything. Lead yourself, lead your superiors, lead your peers, and free your people to do the same. All else is trivia.[11]

The following chapter continues the exploration of why the Impostors underperform and focuses on how they are exposed by the fact that they lack the ability to apply some of the critical skills of leadership.

Notes

1 'Daly Recalls Time He Asked Tiger to Join Him for a Beer.' Golf Channel Digital. April 27, 2016. www.golfchannel.com/article/golf-central-blog/daly-recalls-time-he-asked-tiger-join-him-beer. Accessed August 18, 2020.
2 John Bingham, 'Caretaker who fell off stepladder sues for £50,000 over "inadequate training."' The Telegraph, online edition. June 16, 2008. www.telegraph.co.uk/news/uknews/2139036/Caretaker-who-fell-off-stepladder-sues-for-50000-over-inadequate-training.html. Accessed August 18, 2020.
3 Alan Coppin and John Barratt, Timeless Management (Basingstoke: Palgrave Macmillan, 2016), p. 25.
4 'Homer Defined,' The Simpsons, season 3, episode 5, directed by Mark Kirkland, aired October 17, 1991, on the Fox Network. https://en.wikipedia.org/wiki/Homer_Defined.

5 Glenn Kessler, 'Recalling Hillary Clinton's Claim of "Landing under Sniper Fire" in Bosnia.' *Washington Post*, online edition. May 23, 2016. www.washingtonp ost.com/news/fact-checker/wp/2016/05/23/recalling-hillary-clintons-claim-of-la nding-under-sniper-fire-in-bosnia. Accessed August 18, 2020.

6 Alan Murray, 'From Iran-Contra to Iraqi Weapons, Just What Is a Lie?' *Wall Street Journal*, online edition. June 15, 2004. www.wsj.com/articles/SB108725188381136854. Accessed August 18, 2020.

7 BrainyQuote. www.brainyquote.com/quotes/steve_jobs_416859. Accessed August 18, 2020.

8 'John F. Kennedy Moon Speech – Rice Stadium, September 12, 1962.' https://er. jsc.nasa.gov/seh/ricetalk.htm. Accessed August 18, 2020.

9 *127 Hours*, directed and produced by Danny Boyle. Fox Searchlight Pictures US, 2010. https://dvd.netflix.com/Movie/127-Hours/70141813.

10 BrainyQuote. www.brainyquote.com/authors/andrew-carnegie-quotes. Accessed August 18, 2020.

11 BrainyQuote. www.brainyquote.com/quotes/dee_hock_285470. Accessed August 18, 2020.

Chapter 8

Exposed by What They Do

Milli Vanilli were on their way to the becoming musical icons.[1] Well, for a fleeting moment they were. The duo with the funny hair styles burst onto the pop scene in the late eighties, topping the charts with such memorable (or is it forgettable) ditties such as 'Blame it on the Rain' and winning a Grammy award as Best New Artist in 1990. They were going places, or so it seemed, except for one slight problem. They lacked some of the basic skills for sustaining a career in the music industry. They could not actually sing, or at least not very well, apparently, nor indeed play any instruments to the standard required.

During a 'live' performance, a jammed tape machine at the back of the stage revealed them to be the pop impostors they were, prompting immediate booing from the audience and a wider backlash in the media after the event. They quickly faded back into obscurity, with tragic consequences for one member of the duo who died in the late 1990s from an apparent drug overdose.

Leading others is somewhat akin to being on a stage. Under the spotlight, a leader's talents, and more importantly, their failings are magnified. There is no hiding place. Although the Impostor Leaders might well try to fool us in how they think, and even as to who they are, sooner or later they give the game away by how they act. They cannot hide from their behavior and actions. Out there in the spotlight, their limitations are exposed for all to see; for them, the tape machine frequently jams. None of us can read minds but we can all tell good performance from bad and Impostors regularly reveal themselves not to be effective leaders because they are only miming when it comes to some basic leadership skills.

As you well know, the array of skills needed to succeed as a leader is substantial, and any skill possessed can in some way be put to good use on the leadership stage. Of course, the reverse is true too and skills gaps quickly become a major liability. Genuine leaders top the charts in my experience because they have a depth and breadth of skills which allows them to both manage and lead. They always have talents across four skill sets (Figure 8.1).

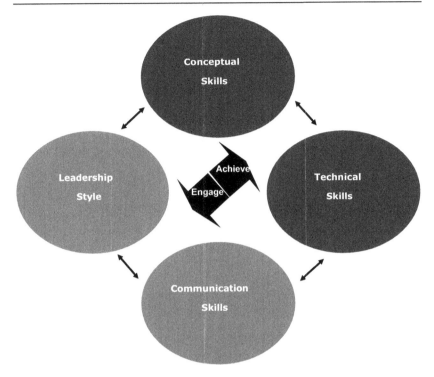

Figure 8.1 Common Skills of Genuine Leaders

Now, it would be laughable to suggest that every Genuine Leader masters all these skills to the same degree, but they do have talents in all these areas:

- **Conceptual.** They can see the big picture and ensure that the organization, or that part of it for which they are responsible, is consistently in tune with a changing operating environment. They are good at recognizing and analyzing complex issues, problem solving, and decision-making.
- **Technical.** They can get to grips with the range of technical skills such as planning or financial management relevant to their level in the organization.
- **Communication.** They can communicate effectively so that they really connect with others.
- **Leadership Style.** They can adjust how they deal with and respond to the roller coaster ride that is life in organizations today.

It would be equally nonsensical to accuse the Impostors of being weak in all these areas. Many are strong on those skills related to the managing aspect of what they do – conceptual and technical – but from what I have seen they always underperform when it comes to the engaging skills.

This chapter shines a spotlight on some of the unforgiveable mistakes that the Impostor Leaders consistently make in how they communicate and in terms of the leadership styles they use. It will highlight how they are essentially paralyzed by their inflexibility. Even though their approaches in these areas frequently do not work, Impostors keep doing the same things over and over. Like mediocre musicians they stick with the playlist long after they have lost their audience. As ever, how they get it wrong will be contrasted against what the Genuine Leaders do well.

What We Have Here Is … Failure to Communicate

The movie buffs among you will surely remember this great line from the classic film *Cool Hand Luke*,[2] a story about a prisoner who refuses to bow to the system. In one powerful scene the evil warden, the Captain, beats Luke, played by Paul Newman, and knocks him to the ground. Then, standing menacingly over him, the Captain utters the memorable words: "What we have here is … failure to communicate."

Impostor Leaders constantly fail to communicate. They just do not get how to do it and I have often felt sorry for them because it causes them all sorts of problems. Instead of mastering its art, they are prone to mutilating it. Their shortcomings as communicators are many and varied but are caused in part from their lack of the supporting personal characteristics such as empathy and assertiveness. They make matters worse for themselves because many Impostors seem oblivious to some of the basic dynamics of interpersonal relations, or indeed how to apply key communication skills.

While the Genuine Leaders usually recognize that effective communication lies at the heart of any positive relationship, the Impostors seem not to grasp this fundamental concept. Yes, they will often be the first to pay lip service to the importance of communication but in practice they are frequently hopeless at it.

Quality Over Quantity

All the Genuine Leaders that I know are great communicators. It is as simple as that. They see the value in regular and structured communication with their people, individually and collectively. But they are less hung up about the quantity of communication than its quality, because they know that the more meetings employees have to attend, or the more time they spend in meetings, the more pressured they are likely to feel. Double those feelings if those meetings are badly run and unproductive. As a result, these leaders make sure that what they do in terms of communication is not only structured and ongoing, but effective too.

The Impostors suffer from a multitude of sins in this regard. Sometimes, I have noticed how they fail to communicate enough, so they fail on the quantity side. For the Deflating Impostors, this is often as a result of their insecurity which leads them to keep face to face communication with their employees, particularly in groups where things might get out of hand, to the minimum required. Toxic Impostors often do not communicate enough simply because when you care so little about people why would you devote more face time to them than was necessary?

Even when Impostors do get the quantity of communication right, its quality is often poor. Former US President George W. Bush was, perhaps unfairly, accused of leading cabinet meetings "like a blind man in a room full of deaf people,"[3] and this is a pretty good way of describing what attending meetings led by the Impostor Leaders is often like:

- Deflating Impostors keep such a tight rein on things at meetings that these events become meaningless as a two-way medium. A classic tactic of Damp Squibs for example is to monopolize the conversation to the extent that this serves to eat up as much of the allocated time as possible, leaving little room for meaningful input from their team. Dark Clouds manage meetings so badly that people usually leave wondering what the hell it was all about.
- Toxic Impostors too fail on the quality side because their meetings are rarely open and interactive events, as who in their right mind is going to really question anything that they say. One employee working for a bully explained the fear when she said to me: "Are you kidding, contradict the boss? You might as well give me the gun now and I'll finish myself off."

Impostors also tend to over rely on written communications. The Deflating Impostors especially can be prolific email and memo writers with the focus being more to cover their own ass than any real belief that this works best. Of course, written forms of communication have their place but there is no substitute for meaningful direct interaction as this comment made to me by one frustrated employee highlights:

We work in an open plan office and my boss actually sits directly opposite me. When she has something awkward to tell me, or if she wants me to do something that she thinks I mightn't like, she always sends me an email. What she doesn't seem to understand is that I am more than happy to do anything she asks, within reason; what makes me so frustrated is that she cannot just look up over the partition and tell me. She drives me absolutely nuts with all her silly emails.

Getting the quantity–quality aspect of communication wrong so frequently contributes to the underperformance seen in the Impostors. But bad as that is, the mistakes they make in how they communicate with others in practice are far worse.

It Ain't What They Say, it's How They Say it

Attention spans are shortening, at least that is what much of the research into this area is telling us.[4] By how much they are falling is open to debate, but a wealth of evidence supports the idea that we are all less able to focus on a given topic now than we were in the past. Whatever the exact span of attention, the ability to concentrate is measured in minutes and this poses significant challenges for all communicators. In the workplace with its multitude of distractions the challenge for leaders to communicate succinctly and effectively is even greater, as there is always a limited window for getting a message across to others. The best leaders know how to make the most of that window.

Genuine Leaders do so because they intuitively understand that how they say things is just as important as what they have to say, in terms of making an impact. They know too that when they communicate with others, be that one or many, the messages flying back and forth have two important elements – *content and context*. They understand that content relates to the words they choose, while context – the emotional part – is about how those words are transmitted and relates to tone and body language. What puts the Genuine Leaders that I encounter head and shoulders above the rest as communicators is that they work hard to always have content and context in alignment. Their style of communication serves to increase the attention span of the listeners and maximizes the retention potential of their messages. They also appreciate that how they receive messages is just as important as how they send them, so they are usually good listeners too.

It is in how they communicate with others that Impostors really show themselves up. They deserve to be booed off the stage for their lack of skill and inflexibility as communicators. For starters, they often surprise me by how little they understand the sender-receiver loop in face-to-face communication, or in how they fail to grasp the emotional dimension to all personal interactions with the result that they get it consistently wrong both in how they send and receive messages. In terms of content side of things, they make lots of mistakes. Former US President Donald Trump provided us with many examples of how he struggled with the content of his messages, some of his statements were simply incoherent. But, for balance, current President Joe Biden has his own issues with content. For sure the negative consequences from failing to get the content of messages right are not just limited to past or current presidents. When any leader communicates, be that with superiors or subordinates, they are essentially taking center stage and are leaving themselves wide open to mockery when they get content wrong, something that the Impostor Leaders frequently do.

Deflating Impostors let themselves down because they are prone to taking too long to get to the point and are usually wafflers, smattering their sentences with badly chosen words, jargon, or meaningless metaphors which push the attention span of their audience to the limits. Recently, while sitting in on an in-company management meeting, the operations manager, a real Damp Squib, used the following terms in the space of thirty minutes:

> As you know we are facing into a mega week with the conference coming up, so it's 'all hands on deck' for the next few days ... I want to make sure we are all singing from the same hymn sheet on this one ... we need to get the team on board ... at the moment there's a bit of cat herding going on ... making a mess of this conference isn't going to happen on my watch.

I mean, please!

As an observer it was interesting to scan the faces on those managers in attendance as they struggled to suppress the urge to snigger, although the furtive glances between one another said it all really. When Abraham Lincoln quipped, "He can compress the most words into the smallest idea of any man I know,"[5] he was surely referring to a Deflating Impostor.

For the Toxic Impostors, particularly the Bullies, it is often the opposite problem and they can come across as too blunt or direct often filling their sentences with coarse or harsh language which is designed to reinforce their generally intimidating natures.

When it comes to content, all the Impostor Leaders overlook simple points like how to construct a message to have maximum positive impact. Yet, the problems with content pale into insignificance when compared to what the Impostors repeatedly do with context. They get this so wrong because they miss the point about the emotional impact of tone and body language; their inflexibility here leads to a lot of bad practices (Figure 8.2).

The cumulative effect of these repetitive, negative behaviors means that for all Impostors, the context of their messages frequently overshadows its content. They do of course have valid things to say, but I have seen that the way they say them weakens or indeed kills the impact. As a result, they do not really reach others at anything other than a surface level. They encourage the listener to tune out not in, losing some or all of the content of their message in the process. A couple of little anecdotes that I picked up from employees emphasize this point well:

> My boss is a real shouter, always having a crisis about something or other. When he does, his face goes purple and a little vein on his

	Deflating Impostors	Toxic Impostors
Tone of Voice	• Too softly spoken • Sounding nervous • Overly apologetic • Mumbling	• Loud • Raised • Shouting • Sarcastic
Eyes	• Uncomfortable making eye contact • Looking down or away a lot	• Staring down • Eyes bulging • Trying to intimidate
Hand Gestures	• Nervous gestures • Fidgeting • Hand wringing	• Lots of pointing • Clenched hands • Thumping table
Body Language	• Inward posture • Obviously uncomfortable • Hunched, self-protecting	• Forward posture • In your face • Leaning • Threatening

Figure 8.2 Common Mistakes Made by Impostors

forehead starts throbbing. It is quite funny actually; we call him the Purple People-Eater when he gets like that: Barney's nasty brother. When he has a go at me now, I just cannot seem to take my eyes of that vein. I miss half of what he's saying because all I'm thinking about is what would happen if it actually burst.

The above came from a manager who was working for a particularly unstable bully, he had found his own escape mechanism. Or take this gem from a guy working for a Damp Squib:

Over the years I've developed the knack of pretending to be interested. I'm pretty good at it now, I have to say. I wish I could put it on my CV but I guess it is not top of the list of things that employers look for. When my boss drones on and on at me, once I get the gist of what she's saying, I drift off somewhere in my head. What's she's saying barely registers – "Blah, blah, blah." But I can make it look like I care. I don't.

Despite first impressions, these two employees were not bad eggs. They were positive characters overall, but they had simply been worn down by prolonged exposure to barrages of context over content from their respective bosses. Naturally, every leader messes up now and again when it comes to communication, but the Impostors get this critical skill wrong more often than right.

Apart from being terrible senders of messages, Impostor Leaders also tend to be poor at receiving them because they are frequently bad listeners too. Not only do they fail to make enough time to listen to people but when they do, they again make some fairly glaring errors, like not making eye contact, constantly interrupting or showing a general disinterest which puts people off.

In my experience, Impostors pay for their shortcomings as communicators at several levels. They cannot build bonds with people to the extent that Genuine Leaders do. It is always much harder, if not impossible, to truly engage people who feel little or no connection to you. The problems do not end there because effective communication is truly the key to everything a leader does and has a direct influence over their ability to apply different leadership styles which is just another form of communication.

To close, good communication is the life blood of effective leadership. Simple as that. And the best leaders have a natural talent for communicating and they follow a simple but golden rule when they do so. The ABC rule: Accuracy, Brevity, and Clarity. Add to this, they have the right personal qualities, such as self-awareness, and the necessary skills which make them really stand out as communicators.

One Size Leadership Style Does Not Fit All

General George S. Patton[6] was a tough, inflexible, and single-minded military hero. Old Blood and Guts, as he was known, is one of the most successful and notorious military leaders in history and played a significant part in the defeat of the Germans in World War II. Patton had an uncompromising leadership style which never changed, and he was known to be direct and stubborn throughout his military career. His bluntness and intolerance were undoubtedly an advantage on the battlefield, but it got him into trouble off it on more than one occasion during his career and nobody earned his wrath more than men he viewed as cowards. In one highly publicized incident, which occurred while he was visiting patients in hospital, he was reprimanded for slapping a soldier who, when asked what was wrong with him, had responded in words to the effect that he was too afraid to fight.

Yet for all of that, Patton cared deeply about the men under his command and generated great loyalty among them because they knew their chances of survival serving under him were greater. In life and death situations, people will always gravitate towards those whom they believe will get them through to the other side, regardless of how they might treat them. In that sense General Patton's inflexible and uncompromising leadership style was a positive, not a negative.

The General would not survive very long in the modern organization. Nor should he be expected to, as leadership is all about time and place. Whereas his rigid and inflexible approach served him well in battle, something more subtle is necessary in the world of work. Organizations are not about life and death, so leaders must have greater flexibility in their approach if they are to handle the nuances and complexities of the today's work environment. Genuine Leaders get this point and have the capacity to deftly adjust their approach in response to different people and situations.

All the Impostors struggle with the flexibility issue. They are not complete automatons, but unlike the Genuine Leaders they tend to have very narrow spans of leadership styles and what they do as leaders is the equivalent of a painter trying to paint a wall by throwing a can of paint at it – they get some coverage but there will be plenty of gaps and a fair amount of mess to clean up afterwards. Their limited styles work for some of their people, some of the time in some situations, but are mostly ineffective when compared against what Genuine Leaders do. Here is a simple example I encountered of how one Impostor could not match their style to the situation:

A new leader was appointed to head a team of twenty designers working in a leading design firm. The previous leader had been in place for several years and had recently left to join a rival firm. Overall, the design team had gained an excellent reputation for creativity and innovation within their industry and had won several awards. The new leader, who had previously been a team member, was appointed because they were the longest serving employee and were seen to be next in line.

The new team leader was eager to establish himself quickly and to prove to the team that he could be just as good as his predecessor. One of the areas that he felt required improvement was how the workload was organized and distributed between the team, as he believed that the designers had too much freedom over how they planned their week. The old system had worked well under the previous leader, but he felt that more structure would be good for everyone.

To address this, he introduced a new reporting system, whereby each designer had to provide a work plan to him at the beginning of every week. Despite protests from the team members, the new leader told them that this was to be the new approach from then on and it would not change, so they should get used to it. In any case, the new leader believed that they would see the benefits of this new system over time.

In making these changes he had hoped to further improve the productivity of the team and the overall quality of their work. However, a month or so after the introduction of the new system, there had been one or two delays in meeting client deadlines, which had rarely occurred before. The team leader felt that this was because a couple of the team members were deliberately slowing down the pace of work and he challenged them about this, which led to a few heated arguments developing. The creative director naturally became aware of this and spoke to the team leader about it, indicating that he expected the situation to be resolved quickly as the company could not afford to upset any of its major clients.

This scenario is but one example of how Impostors tend to apply the wrong leadership style in given situations. Obviously, there is nothing wrong for a new leader in trying to stamp their authority on the position, but there is more than one way to skin a cat as they say. Attempting to railroad new approaches through with an experienced, competent, and relatively high performing team is clearly not the way to go.

This little scenario is symptomatic of the wider problems that Impostor Leaders face when it comes to leadership style. In the first instance, they seem not to realize that the one-size-fits-all approach does not work, particularly today but, what hinders them more is that they also lack the capacity for greater flexibility because of their weaknesses with regard to other elements of the right stuff. This is where their poor self-awareness, negative mindsets, and lack of skills, particularly communication, come home to roost. The knock-on effect of not having the right stuff means they can only confidently operate within their 'comfort zone' in how they lead people every day and his tends to manifest itself in very limited styles of leadership.

Three Leadership Styles

Genuine Leaders, by contrast, do have the solid foundation in place which gives them a platform for being more flexible and responsive to people and events. They know that balancing our work equation requires them to juggle opposing forces which determine the best leadership style to apply in any given circumstance (Figure 8.3).

Impostors, on the other hand, miss the point that leadership styles must change depending upon the levels of direction and control required versus the

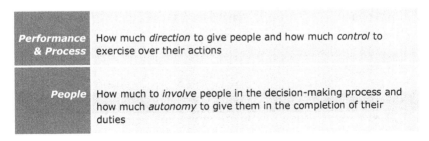

Figure 8.3 Direction and Control versus Involvement and Autonomy

amount of involvement and autonomy to allow employees. No single style, or narrow range of styles, is going to get that balance right. Only flexibility can do it. I have witnessed Genuine Leaders responding differently, in terms of the leadership style they adopted, depending upon issues like:

- *Employee engagement levels*: how engaged employees are will influence their style.
- *Individual performance*: the ability and/or willingness of an individual to deliver what is expected of them will always determine how they respond.
- *Situations/events/problems*: different situations, events and problems will, they know, require different responses.

This means that Genuine Leaders broadly use three different styles of leadership (Figure 8.4).

These are not styles that Genuine Leaders rigidly jump in and out of. It is more a matter of a continuum which they subtly shift back and forth along depending on what they feel will work best. They might use all of these styles in any given day depending upon what they are faced with:

- **Steering.** At times, Genuine Leaders need to exercise high direction and control over their whole team, or on individuals within it. They must 'steer' them in the direction they want them to go. It is an essential style when faced with individual or collective underperformance, when quick decisions or action is required or indeed when decisions must be implemented which are not open to debate. It does not mean being aggressive though – aggression never forms part of the Genuine Leader's approach – but they will be firm and direct as required.

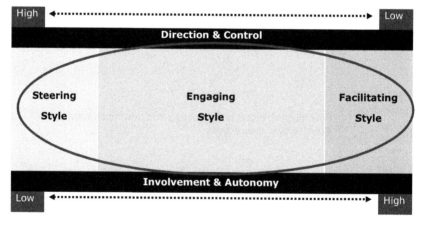

Figure 8.4 Three Styles of Leadership used by Genuine Leaders

- **Engaging.** Genuine Leaders strive to reduce direction and control and increase involvement and autonomy because they know failure to do so only creates employees who act like robots – they will not use their own initiative. They apply this style in simple ways by including people in decision making or in allowing them to propose solutions to given problems. For most of the time, Genuine Leaders try to adopt the engaging style because they know by its very nature it helps to build the engagement levels of employees.
- **Facilitating.** On other occasions, particularly with high performing teams or individuals, Genuine Leaders are willing to give them high levels of involvement and autonomy. As leaders, they take a big step backwards and trust their people to make the right moves. They are still in charge of course but they recognize that their people are ready to be essentially self-leading.

What makes Genuine Leaders so much better as leaders is this ability to be flexible, plus they have the attributes and skills which help them do it well. It would be wrong to say that the Impostors are not flexible to any degree, just not flexible enough. Particularly when feeling under pressure, the Impostors quickly rush back to their comfort zone and many of the approaches they use are to be found at the extremes of the continuum.

Damp Squibs, as we said repeatedly, tend to overdo the direction and control. At their worst, their comfort zone preference is for using a *Controlling* style of leadership (Figure 8.5).

Even when they loosen up a little bit, they rarely shift beyond steering or low engaging styles and therefore they are frequently accused of being micro-managers. In general, their passivity and desire to control limits their

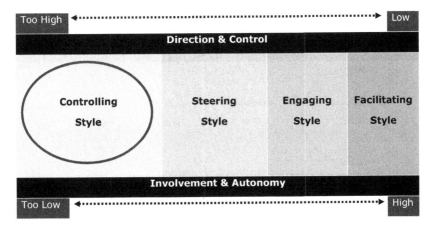

Figure 8.5 An Emphasis on Control

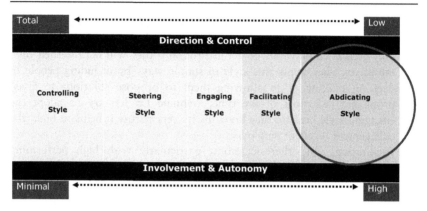

Figure 8.6 Abdicating Leadership Responsibility

ability to be more adaptable. Certainly, they rarely get to high engaging or facilitation styles for to do so would be bad for their blood pressure.

Dark Clouds are hard to slot into the continuum because I believe that they do not really lead at all. They never give enough direction or control and rather than allow involvement and autonomy, they leave people to their own devices a lot of them time, so in essence their predominant style could be described as *Abdicating* (Figure 8.6).

They do of course use other styles but never engaging or facilitating to the level required.

Plotting the Toxic Impostors on the continuum is relatively straightforward. Both Egotists and Bullies have approaches which seek to dominate others so their style most of the time could be described as *Domineering* (Figure 8.7).

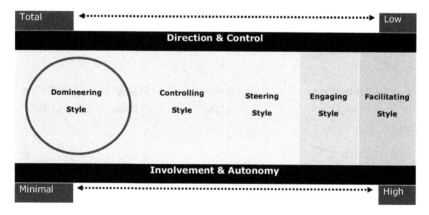

Figure 8.7 Domineering Style of Leadership

The Domineering style is differentiated from a Controlling one in that the Toxic Impostors, particularly the Bullies, apply a lot of aggression in their approach, so their style becomes quite unpleasant for everyone around them. That is not to say that these leaders do not use other styles, but any shift is usually as far as low engaging at best, they always need to feel they are in control. Most of the time these leaders are not interested or indeed comfortable in seeking to broaden their approach.

As one Genuine Leader put it to me: "I am a bit like a chameleon and try to adapt my style to fit the situation I am faced with." In that sense, they make conscious – and that word is important – decisions as to what leadership is going to work best based on the scenario facing them. Unfortunately, the Impostors are more like charlatans than chameleons.

Summary

Being predictable at anything is never a good idea. It is even less advisable in a leadership context. Unfortunately for all the Impostors, that is precisely what they are. Their weaknesses, both in how they communicate and in their over-reliance on a few leadership styles, mean that they are very limited as leaders on a day-to-day basis. It is not that hard to figure out how they are going to react.

Genuine Leaders have all the right attributes and skills which allows them to be flexible in their approach. Impostors are not that nimble and when the proverbial hammer does not work, they only know how to reach for a bigger hammer. The longer they retain this inflexibility, the harder it is for them to break the cycle and they become conditioned to act and behave in ever more uniform ways. Unlike good wine, they get worse with age.

The combined effect of having a range of weaknesses across all elements of the right stuff means that the Impostors struggle as leaders, causing them to consistently underperform and underachieve in comparison to Genuine Leaders. For all the hype surrounding leadership, it is often forgotten that at a fundamental level it is essentially about people leading other people. When an individual does not have the right mindset, has weaknesses across personal characteristics, or suffers from certain skills gaps, it should come as no surprise that they fail the leadership challenge more often than they get it right. When someone lacks the necessary resources to make it as a Genuine Leader, we should not be shocked when they act like an Impostor most of the time. The only surprise is that the Impostor Leaders get so little attention in all that has been written and spoken about how best to lead others.

Notes

1 'Milli Vanilli.' Wikipedia. Last modified August 8, 2020. https://en.wikipedia.org/wiki/Milli_Vanilli. Accessed August 18, 2020.

2 *Cool Hand Luke*, directed by Stuart Rosenberg, Warner Bros–Seven Arts, 1967. http s://dvd.netflix.com/Movie/Cool-Hand-Luke/397323.
3 'Cabinet Members Defend Bush from O'Neill.' CNN, online edition. January 12, 2004. https://edition.cnn.com/2004/ALLPOLITICS/01/11/oneill.bush. Accessed August 18, 2020.
4 Simon Maybin, 'Busting the Attention Span Myth.' BBC News, online edition. March 10, 2017. www.bbc.com/news/health-38896790. Accessed August 18, 2020.
5 Quotes.net. www.quotes.net/quote/2436. Accessed August 18, 2020.
6 'George S. Patton.' Wikipedia. Last modified August 9, 2020. https://en.wikipedia. org/wiki/George_S._Patton. Accessed August 18, 2020.

Conclusion

Looking to the Future

All leaders mess up now and again. This book has not been about those infrequent lapses or occasional misdemeanors. Instead, the focus was on those individuals who consistently get leadership wrong. It explored who these Impostor Leaders were, and how and why they continually underachieve. Their many failings were considered in the light of the strengths seen in Genuine Leaders.

A key message from the book has been that 'leadership' is about managing *and* leading, and that only the very best – the Genuine Leaders – have the talent to do it well. That does not mean they are superheroes; yes, they outshine others, but anyone who is willing to work hard at self-development can rise towards the level of genuine leadership. The intention here has not been to teach, or indeed to promote the view that there is only one right way to lead. It is more a case of there being better and worse ways of doing it. The purpose of exploring the world of the Impostors was to provide you with a chance to reflect on your own performance against the backdrop of how some leaders miss the mark.

Having read the book, maybe you have now identified some Impostor-type failings in yourself. Congratulations, you are human. Do start to get worried, though, if those failings are seen more frequently than your strengths – you are advancing into Impostor territory. What you do with these insights is of course entirely up to you, but standing still should never be the preferred choice. For certain, it would not be the option taken by a Genuine Leader. Is it possible to improve your performance? Absolutely, it is. Is that change likely to be easy? Absolutely not, and even less so if it relates to aspects of the right stuff like increasing self-awareness, changing mindsets, or building personal characteristics. Whatever you decide to do, consider the following question: would you be happy if those around you thought of you as an Impostor Leader?

Only you can get in touch with your inner Impostor and only you can do something about it. In doing so, you must view your progress as a journey, a career-long one. Do not make the mistake that a few training courses, or books, will provide the answer. On their own they will not. Enhancing the

Genuine Leader in you will require a concerted effort over the long term, one that is based upon addressing identified shortcomings and understanding how to put them right. To assist you on that journey, identify people who can guide you, particularly those you believe fit the profile of a genuine leader. Coaching and mentoring will be vital resources as you seek to build your capabilities so do not be afraid to ask for help, that of itself is a sign that you have what it takes for genuine leadership. At all times, recognize that a desire to change and following through on that are two different things entirely. We all make New Year's resolutions, but how many do we stick with beyond February?

On the flip side of the coin, if you are responsible for an Impostor Leader, the good news is that it is possible to change them, or more accurately, for them to change if there is a real desire on their behalf to do so. However, just as applies to your own development, it should be clear that even with a real commitment on their behalf to overcome their shortcomings, it cannot happen overnight, nor will it happen at all unless there is a planned support mechanism put in place. Some key factors to consider in terms of how to deal with an Impostor for whom you are responsible (these next points can also guide your own development):

- **Acceptance.** Nothing can change unless the Impostor recognizes that there is a problem in the first place. Your initial concern should therefore be in helping them to identify that they have performance problems. That can be the biggest challenge and requires effective coaching skills.
- **Ownership.** Not only must the Impostor accept that they have a problem, but they must then take real ownership for the situation. Often Impostors might admit failings in one breath and then in the next will try to weasel out by blaming external forces. Part of this ownership should involve getting the Impostor to identify steps and supports that can help them to change.
- **Set goals.** Like any personal development activity, change should never be an open-ended process so in order to provide focus for the Impostor, clear goals with realistic timeframes should be agreed whereby they must demonstrate progress by defined intervals.
- **Coach and mentor.** As mentioned in relation to your own development, it is important for the Impostor to have access to coaching and mentoring to ensure that they continue to work towards the agreed goals.
- **Recognize achievement.** When an Impostor does show signs of improvement, it is important to recognize their effort which in turn provides them with the motivation to keep going. Equally, if they fail to make the necessary effort, then they should not be tolerated indefinitely within the organization for all the reasons outlined in this book.

The emphasis here has intentionally not been about coping strategies for dealing with life under Impostor Leaders. That is for another day. If you are currently working for one, hopefully you will at least understand that the faults probably lie with them, not you. Take some solace in knowing that you now see right through them for who they really are. It is unlikely you can ever change your boss, but you can at least learn from their mistakes and not repeat them. It would be great if we could make the Impostors pay for their actions, but that is not likely to happen either.

Finally, any journey towards genuine leadership begins with a clear understanding of what makes you tick, what is going on inside you. Hopefully, this book has helped you reflect on that, in the light of what to do and what not to do, and that you can apply those lessons on your journey.

I wish you all the best for the future!

About the Author

Enda Larkin is an entrepreneur, manager, consultant, and author with over 30 years' international experience across multiple business sectors. With a background in hospitality management, where he held several senior posts, he is currently founder and managing director of Dobiquity (www.dobi

quity.com), an online quality management platform with a global client base. Prior to that he ran his own consulting company, HTC Consulting, and managed diverse projects in Ireland, UK, Europe, and the Middle East. He holds a BSc in Management from Trinity College Dublin and an MBA from ESCP Europe in Paris.

He is author of *Ready to Lead?* (Pearson/Prentice Hall, 2007); *How to Run a Great Hotel* (How to Books, 2009); *Quick Win Leadership* (Oak Tree Press, 2011); *Journeys: Short Stories and Tall Tales for Managers* (Oak Tree Press, 2012); and *The Essential Manager: 30 Core Elements of Leadership* (CAI, 2013).

His first novel, *Into the Fire*, was published in 2020 and he writes a regular blog, Work, Life ... and Stories, at www.endalarkin.net.

He is proud father to his wonderful daughters: Keeva and Emily.

Index

Printed in the United States
By Bookmasters